CAROL FOSTER

A FIRESIDE BOOK

PUBLISHED BY SIMON & SCHUSTER

NEW YORK   LONDON   TORONTO

SYDNEY   TOKYO   SINGAPORE

COOKING

WITH

COFFEE

FIRESIDE

SIMON & SCHUSTER BUILDING

ROCKEFELLER CENTER

1230 AVENUE OF THE AMERICAS

NEW YORK, NEW YORK 10020

DESIGNED BY BONNI LEON

MANUFACTURED IN THE UNITED STATES OF AMERICA

1   3   5   7   9   10   8   6   4   2

LIBRARY OF CONGRESS CATALOGING IN PUBLICATION DATA

FOSTER, CAROL, DATE.

COOKING WITH COFFEE / BY CAROL FOSTER.

P.   CM.

"A FIRESIDE BOOK."

INCLUDES INDEX.

1. COOKERY (COFFEE)   I. TITLE.

TX819.C6F67   1992

641.6'373—DC20   91-36433

CIP

ISBN: 0-671-75338-X

To my mother,

Wynnis Perkerson,

with love and

admiration,

for being mother

and father,

and for handling

both roles

with grace.

ACKNOWLEDGMENTS

To Kevin Knox of Starbucks, without whose initial enthusiasm this book would still be an idea. Thank you for your advice, expertise, and continued support.

To Joan Cassidy, Executive Director, and Tim Castle, President, of the Specialty Coffee Association of America, and to Sue Hatch of Seattle's Best Coffee, for support on request.

To Marian Salzman for her pinpoint guidance and generous advice, even when facing her own imminent deadlines.

To Peter Miller and Anthony Schneider, for their professional, no-nonsense way of making this more than a pile of paper.

To Betsy Radin, for making the process of publishing a pleasure.

To Susan Fowler, formerly of Kitchen Kitchen, for her unwavering optimism and infectious sense of humor.

To my stepsons, Tim and Howard, whose computer knowledge and patience go way beyond the call of duty.

And special thanks to my husband, Warren, without whose enthusiasm for fine food I would still be eating hot dogs and yogurt; without whose companionship, generosity, and love, my life would be empty.

CONTENTS

INTRODUCTION

COOKING WITH COFFEE

Coffee packs a room with heady aroma. Its complexity rivals that of fine wine, and its depth of flavor enhances food of all sorts.

Coffee in America has undergone a dramatic transformation in the last twenty years. Consumers are seeking dark, hearty, rich brews, which Europeans have appreciated for decades. Just as we are learning the complexities of wine in drinking and cooking, we are pursuing the diverse pleasures of coffee.

The purpose of this book is to expose the cook to exciting ways of cooking with coffee. Some are common, many are unique. Knowing what makes good coffee is vital to using it in cooking. Just as an unpalatable wine will ruin food, so will a bad brew of coffee. Any dish will be only as tasty as the quality of the ingredients that go into it, so it pays to buy and brew only the best.

While providing intense flavor, even the most expensive coffee is economical relative to other foods. Low in calories and nonalcoholic, coffee is a gastronomic bargain in terms of dollars and calories.

Coffee is assertive enough to marry with strong flavorings such as chocolate, spices, spirits, nuts, and fruits. In many instances, it's used to enhance an ingredient such as chocolate without dominating it.

A brief description of different methods for using coffee in recipes follows. Some are interchangeable, and some can be used in combination.

FRESHLY BREWED COFFEE is the ideal coffee flavoring. Similar to wine, when it's perfect to drink, it's best for cooking. To use brewed coffee, recipes have to accommodate substantial liquid. Brewing coffee double strength—using twice the amount of coffee for the same amount of water—or using brewed espresso will deliver greater coffee flavor than single-strength brewed coffee.

COFFEE CONCENTRATE is an infusion of ground coffee in cold water that's left to "brew" twelve to twenty-four hours and then strained. It is ideal when a dish cannot absorb a lot of liquid. On the other hand, the concentrate can always be diluted to equal the strength of brewed coffee.

COFFEE BEANS—whole, crushed, or ground—provide a new dimension in cooking, although chocolate-covered coffee beans, available from specialty shops, have been used in cake decorating for years. Plain beans make a distinctive ingredient in drinks (Lucky Sambuca, page 48), cookies (Spiced Hazelnut-Chocolate Biscotti, page 126), candy (Almond-Coffee Toffee, page 116), and cakes (Turkish Decadence, page 142).

Beans also flavor liquids, such as milk or cream, that are used in numerous recipes (Espresso Ice Cream, page 134, Chocolate-Espresso Truffles, page 118). The beans steep for a designated time, releasing their flavor, and are then strained from the liquid. After some experimenting, you can vary the amount of steeping time according to your tastes.

LIQUEURS are sweet and alcohol based. Since alcohol lowers the freezing point of food, ice creams and other frozen desserts flavored with liqueurs will remain soft and pliable (Frozen Tia Maria Terrine, page 136). Kamora, Tia Maria, and Kahlúa, the sweetest of the three, are commonly available coffee-flavored liqueurs.

EXTRACTS are also alcohol based. Since alcohol evaporates when heated at low temperatures, extracts do not retain their full flavor when baked. Coffee concentrate is a reasonable substitute, although proportions will vary. If substituting coffee concentrate for an extract, steep the concentrate for a full twenty-four hours.

INSTANT POWDERS are valuable when a recipe has no room at all for liquid, but due to their bitterness, they should be avoided when possible.

BEAN BASICS

offee is a complicated commodity. Two beans from the same branch of the same tree can taste entirely different, depending upon their treatment from tree to cup.

Similar to the grapes that produce wine, coffee beans are greatly influenced by soil conditions, altitude, rainfall, temperature, and their degree of ripeness when picked. Coffee beans benefit from long, cool, slow growth in high altitudes where they have prolonged time to develop. The less hardy species produce more complex, distinct drinks.

There are only two types of coffee beans valuable commercially: arabica and robusta.

Arabica beans have superior flavor, aroma, and richness. They are hard in texture and contain half the caffeine of robustas. Arabicas are difficult to grow, preferring high altitudes, heavy rainfall, and ample shade. Anything called specialty coffee, according to industry practice, includes only arabica beans.

Robusta beans are smaller, rounder, and softer than arabicas. This species is hardy and resistant to disease, and it can be grown at lower altitudes. These qualities make it an easier bean to grow and pick, so it is a less expensive product. Its flavor is harsh or neutral at best, and when roasted, the beans release a cereal-like aroma. Instant coffee is almost 100 percent robusta-based, and vacuum-packed and supermarket blends typically contain large amounts of robusta beans.

Beans may be named for the location where they were grown, the way they were blended or roasted, or just the whim of the purveyor. *South American* and *Central American* beans deliver lively, clean flavor with light to medium body. Their consistency makes them a popular choice and a valuable basis for blended beans. In sharp contrast, *Indonesian* beans offer full body and depth of flavor. They are usually smooth, low in acidity, and earthy. *East African* beans have medium to full body and pleasing acidity. Some offer floral or winy aromas.

Beans are sometimes sold in their pure form, but often they're blended to combine varietal qualities. The professional blender can attain greater complexity and completeness than most pure beans give. Blends may take the name of a pure bean, a style of coffee, or one that's completely contrived. They will vary from store to store and sometimes from season to season.

Labels come and go. Their only value is in pinpointing the coffee that suits each customer's taste.

The taste of coffee can be broken down into four components: aroma, acidity, body, and flavor.

AROMA lures our noses immediately. The aroma lost to the air, however, cannot be recaptured in the cup where it belongs. This is one reason brewing immediately after grinding is critical. Experts describe aroma as delicate, moderate, strong, lacking, faint, fragrant, rich, complex, or distinctive in character.

ACIDITY in coffee denotes a pleasing, cleansing tartness, and does not refer to sourness or pH factors. Just as in a well-balanced wine, acidity in coffee is the lively, refreshing essence of the beverage. Experts refer to coffee acidity as "wininess." Without it, the beverage tastes flat. In cooking, acidity is a key component of flavor, providing balance and piquancy.

Light roasting highlights coffee beans' inherent acidity, since it decomposes fewer of the acids than darker roasting. Medium roasting provides greater body and sweetness. Dark roasting eliminates acidity almost entirely, replacing it with smoky, roasty flavor notes.

BODY provides texture and heaviness. It is the feel of coffee on the mouth. Experts refer to body as watery, slight, light, heavy, full bodied, medium, thin, oily, buttery, smooth, and chewy. The ideal cup of coffee delivers taste that lingers. Compare ice cream to a fruit sorbet or custard to a soufflé and you have the tactile impression of body.

FLAVOR refers to the total character a coffee delivers, including aroma, acidity, and body. Overall coffee flavor is often described as mild, full, mellow, harsh, or distinctive. As in describing wines, flavor also may refer to specific underlying tastes, such as spice, chocolate, nuts, earth, straw, rubber, or grass.

ROASTS AND BLENDS

All but diehard purists leave roasting to the professionals. The expert smells roasting beans for good aroma, tastes them for full flavor development, and checks them for surface color and uniformity.

Commercially, beans are roasted at 400 to 500 degrees for a short period of time, then cooled mechanically. The decrease or delay of a few seconds of roasting time can be critical.

Two beans from the same tree, grown under the same conditions, can take on very different attributes when roasted. Darker roasting results in fuller flavor and less acid in coffee. It also masks the flaws in some lower-grade beans and reduces the amount of caffeine.

The darkness of the roast, however, does not affect the strength of the brew. Strength comes first and foremost from the ratio of grounds to water. The fineness of the grind and the length of contact with water are other determining factors.

Blending is usually done before roasting. An expert evaluates the bean to determine its key attributes. For instance, one type of bean may have good body but little acidity. The professional will use another bean to boost acidity to a desirable level. The goal of blending is to supply a reliable, quality product despite many changing factors, such as weather and soil conditions.

Blending is easy to experiment with at home, although the professionals are on top of the subtle changes in beans from month to month.

Once you know the key characteristics of beans and roasts, you can create your own favorite.

Labels for roasts differ by locality and by retailer. Although roasters routinely distinguish between six or so different degrees of roasting, unfortunately they don't agree on naming them. There is a complete lack of standardization in the dark roast categories.

LIGHT/LIGHT OR HALF CITY/PALE/CINNAMON ROASTS are best suited for mild beans, resulting in a light-brown color, enhanced acidity, dry texture, and delicate flavor and aroma.

AMERICAN/CITY/REGULAR ROASTS are the most common in the United States. This treatment results in medium-brown color, a dry surface, and a flat but sweeter, richer flavor than light roasting.

FULL CITY/FULL/HIGH ROASTS produce dark-brown beans with no oil on the surface. They are less acidic than light roast beans and result in a deep, hearty cup.

VIENNA/FRENCH/ITALIAN/ESPRESSO ROASTS vary by name across the country. The darker the roast, the less acidity and the more oil on the surface of the bean. Dark roasting also reduces the amount of caffeine by small amounts. Most dark roasts are full bodied, rich, and packed with bite. Many have caramel, smoky, or spicy overtones.

GRINDS AND BREWS

A ssuming that you've bought good-quality, fresh beans to brew, you'll want to make the best of them. Just as a cook can burn toast or overcook a steak, top-quality, perfectly roasted beans lose all their potential by careless handling.

Most of the skilled work has been done for the coffee drinker. The beans have been grown, picked, blended, and roasted by professionals. Finding a brewing method you like is up to you.

There are only two basic methods of brewing: boiling and infusion. Infusion is preferred worldwide. Here is a brief description of variously popular brewing methods and equipment.

THE OPEN POT, JUG, **OR** *CAMPFIRE* method of brewing is the oldest and simplest. Pour hot water into a warmed pot filled with coarsely ground coffee. Stir, cover, and leave to infuse 4 to 6 minutes. A small amount of cold water, eggshells, egg whites, or good old-fashioned gravity can be used to settle the grounds. Strain the coffee into a warm cup.

THE PLUNGER, MELIOR, **OR** *CAFETIÈRE* is an adaptation of the jug method. The heat-proof glass jar fitted with a metal plunger or perforated metal filter and lid allows for attractive tabletop brewing. Place ground coffee in the prewarmed plunger, pour in hot water, and replace the filter/lid. The lid helps keep the grounds in contact with the water and keeps the brew warm. After infusing 4 to 5 minutes, carefully lower the plunger. The grounds are forced to the bottom of the jar, and the coffee can be poured from the top.

THE DRIP method requires a heat-proof pot with a removeable lid and a cone to hold a paper or metal filter. Preheat the pot, line the cone with the filter, and place it over the pot. If using a paper filter, wet it slightly first. Place ground coffee in the filter and pour just-boiled water slowly over the grounds. When the water has filtered through, replace the cone with the pot lid. Always opt for porcelain, glass, or stainless steel pots. Aluminum ones tend to transmit a metallic taste.

AUTOMATIC DRIP OR *FILTER MACHINES* regulate the brewing process. Ideally, they heat the water to the correct temperature, time its flow through the grounds, shut off the water's heat source when finished brewing, and turn on an electric plate to maintain the coffee at optimum standing temperature. When buying an electric coffeemaker, be sure that it will hold the proper amount of coffee per cup, that it will heat water to the ideal brewing temperature, and that the cup markings equal 6 ounces each.

THE NEAPOLITAN FLIP OR *MACHINETTA* is an Italian version of a drip pot made up of two compartments with a double filter in the middle. Pour water in the lower tier, fill the center basket with ground coffee, and screw on the top serving section, which has a pouring spout. Place the lower tier over heat to bring the water to a boil. Steam will vent from a valve below the coffee basket when the water is ready. Flip the machinetta over to allow the water to seep through the grounds into the serving container.

THE VACUUM **OR** *GLASS BALLOON,* once quite fashionable, is another attractive, tableside method of brewing coffee. It consists of two glass bowls separated by a stem and filter. Place the ground coffee in the filter in the upper bowl, fill the lower one with cold water, and twist the bowls to create a seal. Heat the lower bowl to create steam pressure, forcing the water through the stem into the upper bowl. Stir the water and grounds, leave for a minute, and remove from the heat. When the coffee has dripped back into the lower bowl, remove the filter and serve the coffee.

ESPRESSO MACHINES produce a dark, concentrated brew quickly. Pressure created by the machine forces steam and water at a high temperature through dark roast, finely ground coffee (see also pages 31–32). To make espresso, use 4 tablespoons of ground coffee to one regular coffee cup (¾ cup or 6 ounces) of water, or double the amount used for regular coffee. Many machines will make cappuccino as well.

PERCOLATORS, whether electric or stove-top, pump boiling water by steam pressure over coffee grounds. They continually recirculate boiling coffee over the used grounds, removing many aroma and flavor components while bringing out the coffee's bitterness.

COFFEE CONCENTRATE is made by infusing cold water with ground coffee, letting it steep for twelve to twenty-four hours, and then straining it through a filter. Special equipment is available to make coffee concentrate, but a large pitcher and fine strainer make an easy home substitute. Time is the key factor in determining the strength of this coffee as opposed to typical brews, in which heat over a short period of time is critical. Although convenient, using coffee concentrate is also expensive, yielding fewer than twenty-five 6-ounce servings per pound of beans. The concentrate can be kept covered and chilled for two weeks. It's perfect for making iced coffees, since ice dilutes beverages. It's also ideal in cooking, since the concentrate delivers maximum flavor with minimum liquid.

To make coffee concentrate, pour 2 quarts of cold water in a container with 1 pound of coffee beans, ground to a medium coarseness. Stir and cover the container. Chill it for twelve hours for a medium-strength concentrate or up to twenty-four hours for a stronger one. After the elapsed time, strain into a clean container and cover until ready to use. Discard the grounds. For quick hot coffee, use 2 tablespoons of concentrate per ¾ cup boiling water. For iced coffee, use 2 tablespoons per ½ cup cold water and add ice.

There are just a few simple rules to follow when brewing at home:

1. STORE BEANS TO PROTECT THEM ADEQUATELY.
Since moisture and air reduce the quality of foods and beverages quickly, place the beans in the smallest possible airtight, moisture-proof container. If using within two weeks, store the container in the refrigerator. If storing for a longer period, freeze the container.

2. GRIND THE BEANS IMMEDIATELY BEFORE BREW-ING. The aroma of freshly ground beans indicates that flavor components are exposed to the air and are lost to evaporation. The sooner water hits ground beans, the more likely those precious aromatic oils will be trapped and on their way to your cup.

3. GRIND THE BEANS EVENLY. Pouring water over a mixture of finely and coarsely ground beans results in unevenly extracted flavor. Overextraction causes bitterness; underextraction causes underdeveloped flavor.

The convenient electric "grinders" available today are not actually grinders; they chop the beans just as a knife would, and are fast, convenient, inexpensive, and easy to clean. Cleanliness is critical, since invisible oils often remain on exposed surfaces and turn rancid over time.

Blenders grind beans adequately and are also easy to clean, but they vary in their efficiency. Timing is essential when using electric machines for grinding, so a fine grind is usually easier to attain in a blender or electric grinder than a coarse one.

4. MATCH THE GRIND TO THE BREWING METHOD. A

great brew is a function of the fineness of the grind and the length of time water is in contact with the grounds. Since a fine grind exposes more surface area of the coffee to the water at once, a shorter brewing time will do. Coarsely ground coffee needs more brewing time to produce the same flavor.

Get to know your coffeemaker. Use a fine grind if your machine takes 1 to 4 minutes to brew, a medium grind for 4 to 6 minutes, and a coarse grind for 6 to 8 minutes.

A *fine grind* is used for espresso and for filtration and drip methods where paper filters are used. Fine grinds slow down the flow of water through them, and they prove to be economical due to high flavor yield.

Drip or *medium grinds* are used for drip pots and vacuum methods.

A *regular* or *coarse grind* is ideal for steeping and percolating. These methods keep water in contact with the grounds for longer periods, and the coarser grind ensures that the grounds can be easily strained.

5. USE ONLY THE BEST WATER. Artificially softened or alkaline

water or that with off tastes, excessive chlorination, or impurities will downgrade the quality of an otherwise perfect beverage. Naturally soft water is ideal. If you live in an area with poor water, consider using filtered or bottled water.

Use fresh cold water, bring it to a boil briefly, and remove it from the heat. Excessive boiling makes water taste flat. Removing the water from the heat brings it to an ideal temperature of 195 to 205 degrees without ticklish temperature measuring. If the water is not hot enough, the aromatic oils will remain in the grounds. If it is too hot, the coffee will be overextracted and bitter.

6. MEASURE THE CORRECT AMOUNT OF COFFEE AND WATER. No matter what the method used to make coffee, the measurements remain the same. Use 2 tablespoons ground beans to one coffee cup (¾ cup or 6 ounces) of water. Espresso or Moka machines may call for double that amount.

7. NEVER ALLOW COFFEE TO BOIL. Choose a coffeemaker that maintains an ideal temperature. Steeping ground beans in water close to the boiling point while never allowing it to boil releases maximum aroma and flavor without producing bitterness. In 185- to 203-degree water, caffeine dissolves. At higher temperatures, the tannin crystals in coffee release bitterness into the brew.

8. DISCARD THE GROUNDS IMMEDIATELY AFTER BREWING. No matter what type of brewing machine you use, remove the grounds as soon as the cycle is complete. Never reuse grounds. Clean the basket or filter as soon as possible to keep residual oils from building up and turning rancid.

9. NEVER REHEAT COFFEE. Avoid violent temperature shifts. Ideally, keep coffee between 185 and 190 degrees for 20 to 30 minutes maximum on a burner. If you must hold coffee longer than thirty minutes, transfer it to a thermos.

BUTTER Use only unsalted butter. Especially in pastries and cakes, even a small amount of salt can be detected.

CHOCOLATE The higher the cocoa butter content of chocolate, the richer and smoother its taste. Many types are interchangeable, but sweetness varies by brand. Store it in a cool dry place, not in the refrigerator. Chocolate should be chopped or grated before melting with very gentle heat.

COCOA POWDER Use only Dutch-process unsweetened cocoa powder. Alkali has been added to it to make it darker and less acidic.

COFFEE Unless specified otherwise, the coffee used in these recipes is a dark roast South American blend. For brewed coffee, use 2 tablespoons ground beans to ¾ cup water; for brewed espresso, use 4 tablespoons ground beans to ¾ cup water under pressure. Espresso or caffè freddo (properly made shots of espresso chilled in an airtight container) and double-strength coffee made in a plunger pot or drip machine are excellent sources of coffee flavor for foods. You may vary the intensity of coffee flavor in most recipes by using a different roast. Use decaffeinated beans if you must, but the amount of caffeine consumed in most foods cooked with coffee is minimal. For dense coffee flavor in desserts, Indonesian coffees provide fullness and earthiness. They give far more body and a richer presence than a simple dark roast. For coffee drinks, especially iced ones, the East African coffees deliver finer aroma than most due to their winy and floral acidity.

CREAM Use heavy whipping cream, containing about 36 percent fat, unless specified otherwise. Before whipping, chill the beaters, bowl, and cream to achieve maximum volume.

EGGS Use large eggs unless specified otherwise. Room-temperature egg whites will whip to a greater volume than cold ones. Freeze extra whites or yolks for future use.

NUTS Roasted nuts have greater flavor, color, and crunch than unroasted ones. Spread whole or chopped nuts in a single layer on a baking sheet. Roast them at 350 degrees 8 to 12 minutes, or until they turn golden brown. Remove from the oven and cool completely before handling.

VINEGAR Balsamic vinegar delivers an intense sweet-tart flavor. It is made in the area around Modena, Italy, from the reduced unfermented juices of Trebbiano grapes. This pricy vinegar is aged for at least six years in wooden barrels. Red wine vinegar can be used as a substitute, but it lacks the fullness of flavor of balsamic. Blueberry vinegar gives a light, fruity aroma. It is available commercially and is easily made at home by steeping berries in good-quality white vinegar.

= O N E =

DRINKS

Countries around the world are famous for their coffee creations. None are more widely acclaimed, however, than Italian specialties. In the 1940s, Achille Gaggia modernized the original steam-pressure espresso machines, and the new brew spread in popularity instantly.

The original machines forced too much steam through ground coffee, producing an overextracted brew. Today's sophisticated electric machines make brewing espresso at home a snap, complete with digital readouts and heated cup racks. The machines force water and steam heated just below the boiling point through finely ground dark roast beans. The result is a syrupy, slightly bitter coffee topped by a thin layer of foam. Espresso delivers pure coffee flavor, and it takes all of 25 seconds to brew.

Some espresso machines also have siphons for foaming milk to make another Italian import, cappuccino. Unfortunately, many espresso machines are expensive, but they provide the only method to use pressure rather than gravity to brew. They also provide the only way to make such a fine, concentrated "cognac of coffee."

Turkish and Mexican coffees are intensely flavored and presweetened. Both are brought to a boil, causing an astringent, potent brew. The Turks use a long-handled metal *ibrik* and the Mexicans use a small earthenware pot, but a heavy saucepan will do for both.

Café au lait, diluted and comforting, is a French breakfast favorite. Equal parts of hot coffee and milk are poured simultaneously into large handleless cups or mugs. It's often used to dip a baguette, brioche, or croissant. Italian caffè latte, Spanish café con leche, and German kaffee milch are milk-and-coffee-based beverages similar to café au lait.

Coffee marries beautifully with spirits of all sorts. Some are simple pairings of coffee and liqueur (usually 1 ounce of liqueur to 1 cup of coffee), many include cream, and others are elaborate flambéed concoctions with spices and fruit. One unique classic is Sambuca, which is traditionally sipped with whole beans floating in it.

TO MAKE ESPRESSO, follow the manufacturer's instructions for your machine. Espresso machines use pressure rather than gravity to brew, thereby providing a more complete extraction of coffee grounds and a greater concentration of solubles than a regular coffee machine. Choose a dark roast bean, usually called espresso or Italian roast. Most machines call for double the amount used to brew regular coffee. Grind it to a fine, powdery, but not flour-like, consistency. You should be able to feel some grittiness in the grounds. Tamp the grounds firmly and evenly in the perforated metal filter. This is a bit of an art and takes some practice. If the grounds are packed too tightly, the water won't be able to drip through; if they're not packed tightly enough, the water will flow through without extracting enough from the grounds. A single espresso is typically made from 7 to 10 grams of coffee, yielding 1 to 1½ ounces of liquid and a thin layer of foam or *crema*, in 18 to 25 seconds. Serve it hot in small cups with a twist of lemon zest.

TO MAKE CAPPUCCINO, blend equal parts brewed espresso, steamed milk, and foamed milk. Pour into warm cups and stir in sugar to taste, if desired. Sprinkling cappuccino with ground cinnamon, nutmeg, or unsweetened cocoa powder is an American innovation, but delicious nonetheless.

TO MAKE CAFÉ AU LAIT, pour equal parts strong-brewed French Roast coffee and hot milk simultaneously into a large cup or small bowl. Vary the proportions to suit your taste.

TO MAKE CAFFÈ LATTE, pour hot espresso and hot steamed milk with little or no foam into warm mugs. If desired, sweeten and sprinkle with freshly grated nutmeg or ground cinnamon.

TO MAKE ICED COFFEE, use a strong brew such as shots of espresso, double-strength coffee, or coffee concentrate. Since the coffee will be diluted and chilled, use beans with a great deal of staying power and flavor interest, such as East African ones. Add sugar to taste, if desired. Cover and chill the coffee in an airtight pitcher, and use it as soon as possible. Add cream or milk, if desired, and ice.

· TURKISH COFFEE ·

T hick, black, and murky with sediment, Turkish coffee is sipped from tiny cups. It's popular not only in Turkey, but throughout the Middle East and parts of Russia. For variety, cloves, cardamom, cinnamon, or nutmeg can be added while dissolving the sugar.

MAKES 3 TO 4 SERVINGS

2 TABLESPOONS SUGAR

1 ½ CUPS WATER

2 TABLESPOONS COFFEE BEANS, GROUND TO A FLOUR-LIKE CONSISTENCY

1 Stir the sugar and water in an *ibrik* or a heavy small saucepan over medium heat until the sugar dissolves. Blend in the coffee and bring the mixture to a boil without stirring.

2 When the coffee froths up to the rim, take it off the heat and let the grounds settle.

3 Repeat the boiling and settling two more times. Pour into demitasse cups. Include a bit of froth for each serving.

• HOT OR ICED ESPRESSO MOCHA •

T his version of hot chocolate makes a hearty breakfast drink or a delicious dessert. Espresso pairs better with chocolate than a weaker brew of coffee—neither flavor is overwhelmed, so both can be relished.

MAKES 4 SERVINGS

4 OUNCES SEMISWEET CHOCO-
   LATE, GRATED
3 CUPS MILK
2 CUPS BREWED ESPRESSO,
   HOT

WHIPPED CREAM (OPTIONAL)
UNSWEETENED COCOA OR
   GROUND CINNAMON
   (OPTIONAL)

1 Place the chocolate and the milk in a heavy medium saucepan over medium heat. Stir occasionally until the chocolate melts. Whisk in the espresso, blending completely.

2 Pour into warm mugs, top with whipped cream, if desired, and dust with cocoa or cinnamon.

3 To make iced mocha, melt the chocolate in the hot espresso. Whisk in the milk, cover, and chill in the refrigerator or place over a bowl of ice water and stir occasionally until cold. Whisk, pour into tall glasses, and add ice, if desired. Top with whipped cream, if using, and dust with cocoa or cinnamon.

• ESPRESSO GRANITA WITH CREAM •

G ranita, an Italian caffè staple, is a coarse-grained ice that dissolves
— slowly in the mouth; its large ice crystals provide satisfying, cooling
chewiness on hot days. For variety, add rum, brandy, or vanilla extract
to the ice before freezing. Be sure to use a dark roast coffee, since freezing
diminishes its flavor, and use the granita the day it's made—the coffee
can become bitter over time. Whipped cream complements its bittersweet flavor.

MAKES 6 SERVINGS

½ CUP SUGAR

1 CUP WATER

2 CUPS BREWED ESPRESSO OR
  DOUBLE-STRENGTH DARK
  ROAST COFFEE

1 CUP CREAM, WHIPPED
  (OPTIONAL)

1 Stir the sugar and water in a heavy small saucepan over low heat
until the sugar dissolves. Simmer without stirring for 5 minutes.

2 Remove from the heat and stir in the espresso. Pour into a shallow
freezer tray. Cool to room temperature and place in the freezer for 30
minutes.

3 Remove from the freezer and blend the ice from the edges of the container into the softer portion of the mixture. Repeat every 30 minutes for 3 to 4 hours or until the granita is evenly frozen and slightly creamy.

4 To serve, spoon the granita into stemmed wine or parfait glasses and top each with a spoonful of whipped cream, if desired.

• BELGIAN ORANGE COFFEE •

C itrus, coffee, and cream team up here for an unbeatable combination. Use Grand Marnier, Triple Sec, or Strega for different nuances in taste—all provide sweetness, fragrance, and lively orange flavor.

MAKES 4 SERVINGS

3 CUPS BREWED DARK ROAST COFFEE, HOT

3 TABLESPOONS SUGAR

¼ TEASPOON GROUND CINNAMON

½ TEASPOON VANILLA EXTRACT

½ CUP ORANGE-FLAVORED LIQUEUR

½ CUP CREAM, LIGHTLY WHIPPED

4 STRIPS ORANGE ZEST

GROUND CINNAMON

1 Blend the coffee, sugar, and cinnamon until the sugar dissolves. Stir in the vanilla extract and orange-flavored liqueur. Pour into 4 warm mugs or coffee glasses.

2 Rest the neck of an inverted spoon over one glass at a time. Slowly pour ¼ of the whipped cream over the back of the spoon to form a floating layer of cream. Do not stir. Repeat for each serving.

3 Top each glass with a strip of orange zest and a sprinkling of cinnamon. Serve immediately.

· VIENNESE COFFEE ·

C lassic Viennese Coffee requires only chocolate, cream, and coffee. The addition of brandy, however, makes a welcome after-dinner or rainy-afternoon treat. Substitute freshly grated orange peel or nutmeg to vary the fragrant optional garnishes.

MAKES 4 SERVINGS

4 OUNCES SEMISWEET OR
  BITTERSWEET CHOCOLATE,
  GRATED
¼ CUP CREAM
4 CUPS BREWED DARK ROAST
  COFFEE, HOT

SUGAR TO TASTE
½ CUP BRANDY (OPTIONAL)
¼ CUP WHIPPED CREAM
COCOA POWDER OR GROUND
  CINNAMON (OPTIONAL)

1 Melt the chocolate with the cream in a heavy small saucepan over low heat. Stir until the mixture is smooth. Blend in the coffee, taste, and add sugar, if desired.

2 Pour into 4 warm cups. Add the brandy for a laced version. Top with whipped cream, and garnish the cream with a dusting of cocoa powder or cinnamon, if desired.

· ICED CAFÉ AU LAIT ·

*U*sing double-strength dark roast coffee and ice cubes made from chilled coffee helps keep iced drinks from diluting. Using half-and-half instead of milk helps this particular drink stay full strength as well.

MAKES 4 SERVINGS

**2 CUPS BREWED DOUBLE-
  STRENGTH DARK ROAST
  COFFEE, CHILLED
2 CUPS MILK OR HALF-AND-
  HALF**

**SUGAR TO TASTE
¼ CUP CREAM, LIGHTLY
  WHIPPED (OPTIONAL)**

1 Divide the chilled coffee and milk or half-and-half evenly among 4 glasses. Stir in the sugar to taste.

2 Fill the glasses with shaved ice and top with lightly whipped cream, if desired.

• MOCHA MILKSHAKE •

*T*he blender makes concocting this adult shake child's play. Add a spoonful of malted milk powder to make a malted mocha shake, or use chocolate syrup instead of chocolate ice cream for a richer taste.

MAKES 2 LARGE DRINKS

4 SMALL SCOOPS COFFEE ICE CREAM OR ESPRESSO ICE CREAM (PAGE 134)

2 SMALL SCOOPS CHOCOLATE ICE CREAM

1 CUP BREWED DARK ROAST COFFEE, CHILLED

½ CUP MILK

COCOA POWDER OR GRATED CHOCOLATE (OPTIONAL)

1 Combine the ice creams, coffee, and milk in a blender. Mix just until smooth.

2 Pour into 2 large chilled glasses and top with cocoa powder or grated chocolate, if desired. Serve immediately with 2 straws and a long-handled spoon in each.

• COFFEE SODA •

B e sure to use fresh brewed, dark roast coffee in iced drinks. Over
time, even when chilled, coffee will taste flat. The dark roast ensures
lots of flavor and aroma when diluted.

MAKES 2 SERVINGS

2 CUPS BREWED DARK ROAST
  COFFEE, CHILLED
1 CUP CLUB SODA
4 SMALL SCOOPS VANILLA ICE
  CREAM

WHIPPED CREAM (OPTIONAL)
FRESHLY GRATED NUTMEG,
  GROUND CINNAMON, OR
  COCOA POWDER (OPTIONAL)

1 Divide the coffee between 2 tall glasses. Pour in half the club soda
and add 2 scoops ice cream to each.

2 Top with whipped cream and a sprinkling of nutmeg, cinnamon, or
cocoa powder, if desired. Serve immediately with 2 straws and a long-
handled spoon in each.

• CAFÉ DE BELGIQUE •

*I*nstead of delicately ladling cream over the back of a spoon, pouring coffee down the side of the glass preserves the layer of lightened cream over this aromatic drink. Sweetening the brew ahead of time eliminates clouding from stirring, as well.

MAKES 4 SERVINGS

½ CUP CREAM
½ TEASPOON VANILLA EXTRACT
1 EGG WHITE, ROOM
  TEMPERATURE

4 CUPS BREWED DARK ROAST
  COFFEE, HOT, SWEETENED TO
  TASTE

1 In a deep, chilled bowl, beat the cream until soft peaks form. Add the vanilla extract and beat another 15 seconds. In a small bowl, beat the egg white until almost stiff. Fold the egg white into the whipped cream.

2 Divide the mixture evenly among 4 stemmed coffee glasses or glass mugs. Pour 1 cup coffee down the side of each glass and serve immediately.

• HOT BUTTERED COFFEE •

A takeoff on classic hot buttered rum, this drink is a warming, lightly
— spiced brew. Make a large batch of the batter, if you like, and store
it in the refrigerator for later use.

MAKES 6 SERVINGS

4 TABLESPOONS UNSALTED
  BUTTER, SOFTENED
1 CUP LIGHTLY PACKED BROWN
  SUGAR
½ TEASPOON GROUND
  CINNAMON
¼ TEASPOON FRESHLY GRATED
  NUTMEG

¼ TEASPOON GROUND
  ALLSPICE
⅛ TEASPOON GROUND CLOVES
6 CUPS BREWED DARK ROAST
  COFFEE, HOT
6 3-INCH CINNAMON STICKS

1 In a small bowl, blend the butter, brown sugar, and ground spices.
If not using immediately, cover tightly and chill.

2 When ready to serve, divide the coffee among 6 warm coffee mugs.
Stir 1 tablespoon batter (or more, to taste) into each mug, and stir until
the sugar dissolves. Top each with a cinnamon stick, and serve immediately.

• ESPRESSO EGGNOG •

*T*his is a light, frothy eggnog, since the egg whites are beaten and incorporated separately. For a smooth instead of fluffy drink, beat the yolks and whites together in step 1.

MAKES 6 SERVINGS

4 EGGS, SEPARATED
¾ CUP SUGAR
2 CUPS MILK
1 CUP BREWED ESPRESSO,
  CHILLED

1 TABLESPOON VANILLA
  EXTRACT
1 CUP CREAM
FRESHLY GRATED NUTMEG

1 In a large bowl, beat the egg yolks and sugar until thick and lemon-colored. Slowly blend in the milk, espresso, and vanilla.

2 In a deep, chilled bowl, beat the cream until it holds soft peaks. Stir into the espresso mixture. Whip the egg whites until almost stiff, and stir into the eggnog. Pour into 6 coffee cups, and sprinkle with nutmeg. Serve immediately.

· ICED ALMOND LATTE ·

*A*lthough almond syrup is most often paired with espresso, use your
favorite flavored syrup in this iced latte. Whip extra syrup into the
cream, if you like, for additional almond flavor.

MAKES 2 SERVINGS

½ CUP BREWED ESPRESSO,
  COLD
1 TO 2 TABLESPOONS ALMOND
  SYRUP
1 CUP MILK

¼ CUP WHIPPED CREAM
  (OPTIONAL)
FRESHLY GRATED NUTMEG
  (OPTIONAL)

1 Divide the espresso and almond syrup between 2 glasses and blend.
Add shaved ice, and fill with cold milk.

2 Top each glass with 2 tablespoons whipped cream and sprinkle with
nutmeg, if desired.

• CAFÉ BRÛLOT •

F estive, fireproof brûlot bowls have been known in New Orleans
— since before 1900. For special drama, flambé the brûlot in a darkened
room, preferably one with a high ceiling. Some restaurants add a flaming
ladle of Cointreau or curaçao just before serving.

MAKES 8 SERVINGS

3 OUNCES BRANDY

3 3-INCH CINNAMON STICKS

10 WHOLE CLOVES

2 TABLESPOONS SUGAR

RIND OF 1 LEMON, CUT INTO
THIN STRIPS

RIND OF 1 ORANGE, CUT INTO
THIN STRIPS

4 CUPS BREWED DARK ROAST
COFFEE, HOT

1 Heat the brandy with the cinnamon, cloves, sugar, lemon rind, and
orange rind to just below boiling in a fireproof brûlot bowl, chafing
dish, or heavy medium saucepan.

2 Carefully ignite with a match and ladle the mixture for about 2
minutes.

3 Stir in the hot coffee and pour immediately into 8 warm demitasse
cups.

· IRISH COFFEE ·

U se a strong brew of coffee when pairing it with liqueurs, since they can overwhelm the taste of coffee. Sipping this warm treat is especially delicious through the cool top layer of rich cream.

MAKES 1 SERVING

1 OUNCE IRISH WHISKEY

2 TEASPOONS SUGAR

4 OUNCES BREWED DARK
ROAST COFFEE, HOT

2 TABLESPOONS LIGHTLY
WHIPPED CREAM

1 Heat the whiskey and sugar in a heavy small saucepan, stirring until the sugar dissolves. Pour into a warm 7-ounce cup or Irish coffee glass. Blend in the coffee.

2 Rest the neck of an inverted spoon over the glass. Slowly pour the whipped cream over the back of the spoon to form a floating layer of cream. Do not stir. Serve immediately.

• LUCKY SAMBUCA •

S ambuca is an Italian liqueur made from anise and sugar. Float an odd number of coffee beans in a liqueur glass filled with Sambuca, crunch the beans between sips, and tradition has it that you will have good luck.

MAKES 1 SERVING

1 OUNCE SAMBUCA   **3 OR 5 COFFEE BEANS**

1 Pour the Sambuca into a liqueur glass and float the beans on top.

2 Ignite the surface with a match and serve immediately. Blow out the flame gently. Between sips of liqueur, eat the coffee beans.

• SPICED-RUM COFFEE •

S ince rum is distilled from sugar cane, its natural sweetness complements coffee. The spices and fruits, such as cinnamon, nutmeg,
cloves, and citrus that we typically pair with coffee, we also pair with
rum. This drink is a warm blend of the best of them.

MAKES 2 SERVINGS

2 CUPS BREWED DARK ROAST
  COFFEE, HOT
2 TABLESPOONS SUGAR OR TO
  TASTE
2 WHOLE CLOVES

2 STRIPS ORANGE ZEST
2 OUNCES DARK RUM
¼ CUP WHIPPED CREAM
FRESHLY GRATED NUTMEG

1 Pour the coffee into 2 warm glass coffee mugs. Add 1 tablespoon
sugar, 1 clove, and 1 strip of orange zest to each, and stir until the sugar
dissolves.

2 Blend 1 ounce rum into each mug, top gently with the whipped
cream, and sprinkle the cream with a bit of nutmeg. Serve immediately.

• MUD SLIDE •

T he "mud" refers to the earthy color of this drink, and the "slide" refers to the ease with which it goes down. Freeze chilled coffee in ice cube trays to keep iced coffee drinks cold without diluting them.

MAKES 2 SERVINGS

2 CUPS BREWED DARK ROAST COFFEE, CHILLED
2 OUNCES COFFEE LIQUEUR
2 OUNCES BAILEYS IRISH CREAM

1 OUNCE VODKA
WHIPPED CREAM, SWEETENED (OPTIONAL)

1 Blend the coffee, the liqueur, the Irish Cream, and the vodka in a cocktail shaker.

2 Fill 2 glasses with shaved ice. Divide the coffee mixture between the glasses, top with whipped cream, if desired, and serve immediately.

· CAFÉ CALYPSO ·

A brandy snifter's tapered shape is elegant and functional, too; it di-
rects every bit of tantalizing aroma to the nose. Serve Café Calypso
in glass coffee cups or stemmed glasses if snifters are unavailable.

MAKES 4 SERVINGS

**4 CUPS BREWED DARK ROAST
  COFFEE
¼ CUP COFFEE LIQUEUR**

**2 TABLESPOONS DARK RUM
⅜ CUP CREAM, LIGHTLY
  WHIPPED**

1 Heat the coffee with the coffee liqueur and rum in a heavy medium
saucepan. Do not allow it to boil. Pour into 4 warm brandy snifters.

2 Rest the neck of an inverted spoon over one glass at a time. Slowly
pour ¼ of the whipped cream over the back of the spoon so that it
floats. Do not stir. Repeat with each glass, and serve immediately.

• JAMAICAN 75 •

*T*he French 75, made of gin, lemon juice, Cointreau, and champagne, — was the model for the Jamaican 75, which uses coffee liqueur instead of gin or Cointreau. Both are potent—the original was named after a French 75 howitzer cannon.

MAKES 2 SERVINGS

2 OUNCES COFFEE LIQUEUR   **10 OUNCES DRY CHAMPAGNE**
2 TEASPOONS FRESH LEMON
  JUICE

1 Divide the coffee liqueur and lemon juice between 2 12-ounce glasses. Stir well.

2 Fill the glasses with shaved ice. Pour 5 ounces champagne into each, stir, and serve immediately.

• COCONUT-COFFEE SMOOTHIE •

T his one's for serious coconut lovers. Add cold brewed coffee, if
desired, to make a lighter, more coffee-flavored drink.

MAKES 2 SERVINGS

4 CUPS ICE

¾ CUP CANNED CREAM OF
  COCONUT

⅜ CUP COFFEE LIQUEUR

⅜ CUP BAILEYS IRISH CREAM

BREWED DARK ROAST COFFEE,
  CHILLED (OPTIONAL)

2 TABLESPOONS GRATED
  SWEETENED COCONUT
  (OPTIONAL)

1 Place the ice, cream of coconut, and the liqueurs in a blender and
mix until smooth. Stir in chilled coffee, if using, to taste.

2 Pour the drink over ice in 2 tall glasses. Sprinkle with coconut, if
desired, and serve immediately.

TWO

BREAKFAST
FARE

• CAPPUCCINO FRENCH TOAST •

*T*ransform leftover French bread into a unique French toast. For those who aren't quite awake by breakfast, the milk and coffee mixture can be prepared the night before. All that's left is to dip and grill.

MAKES 4 SERVINGS

2 EGGS

¼ CUP MILK

¼ CUP BREWED DARK ROAST COFFEE, COOLED SLIGHTLY

2 TABLESPOONS LIGHTLY PACKED BROWN SUGAR

2 TABLESPOONS COFFEE LIQUEUR

¼ TEASPOON GROUND CINNAMON

¼ TEASPOON FRESHLY GRATED NUTMEG

4 SLICES WHITE BREAD, PREFERABLY 1 TO 2 DAYS OLD

3 TABLESPOONS UNSALTED BUTTER

2 SLIGHTLY UNDERRIPE BANANAS, SLICED LENGTHWISE (OPTIONAL)

MAPLE SYRUP (OPTIONAL)

1 In a medium bowl, whisk the eggs, milk, coffee, sugar, coffee liqueur, cinnamon, and nutmeg. Pour into a pie plate or shallow dish. Trim the crusts from the bread, if desired. Soak two slices of bread in the egg mixture 2 to 3 minutes. Turn over and let soak on the other side briefly.

2 Heat 1 tablespoon butter in a heavy 9-inch skillet. Drain the bread slightly and fry over medium-high heat until golden on each side. Remove to a warm oven. Repeat with the remaining two slices.

3 Heat the remaining tablespoon of butter. When bubbling, sauté the banana slices, if using, on both sides about 2 minutes, or just until lightly browned. Serve the toast and bananas with warm maple syrup, if desired.

· CRÊPES CAFÉ AU LAIT ·

E qual parts of coffee and milk distinguish these crêpes from the ordinary. Serve them for breakfast with maple syrup, or make larger ones for dessert and serve with whipped cream and fruit.

MAKES 20 4-INCH CRÊPES

¾ CUP ALL-PURPOSE FLOUR

2 TABLESPOONS SUGAR

1 TEASPOON BAKING POWDER

¼ TEASPOON SALT

2 LARGE EGGS, BEATEN

½ CUP MILK

½ CUP BREWED DARK ROAST
  COFFEE, COOLED SLIGHTLY

1 TEASPOON VANILLA EXTRACT

2 TABLESPOONS COFFEE
  LIQUEUR (OPTIONAL)

2 TABLESPOONS UNSALTED
  BUTTER, MELTED

UNSALTED BUTTER, MELTED

MAPLE SYRUP

1 Sift the flour with the sugar, baking powder, and salt into a medium bowl.

2 Blend the eggs with the milk, coffee, vanilla, coffee liqueur, if using, and 2 tablespoons melted butter. Make a well in the center of the flour mixture. Pour in the liquid ingredients, and blend lightly with a few strokes. The batter should be the consistency of heavy cream. Strain, if necessary, to make the batter perfectly smooth.

3 Heat a large skillet or, preferably, a griddle over medium heat. Spread a small amount of butter over the cooking surface. When the foam from the butter subsides, slowly pour the batter onto the griddle, forming 4-inch circles.

4 Cook until bubbles appear on the crêpes. Turn with a spatula and cook the other side until lightly browned. Serve with melted butter and warm maple syrup.

· KONA COCONUT MUFFINS ·

*J*ust a hint of coffee enhances this delicious combination of coconut and walnuts. Substitute macadamias, if you like, for a really rich breakfast treat.

MAKES 12 MUFFINS

½ CUP UNSALTED BUTTER, ROOM TEMPERATURE

½ CUP SUGAR

½ CUP LIGHTLY PACKED BROWN SUGAR

2 EGGS

1¾ CUPS ALL-PURPOSE FLOUR

1 TABLESPOON BAKING POWDER

¼ TEASPOON SALT

½ CUP BREWED DARK ROAST COFFEE, COOLED SLIGHTLY

⅓ CUP MILK

2 TEASPOONS VANILLA EXTRACT

1½ CUPS COARSELY CHOPPED WALNUTS

¾ CUP SWEETENED GRATED COCONUT

1 Preheat the oven to 350 degrees. Grease and flour 12 muffin cups or line them with paper baking cups.

2 In a large bowl, cream the butter with the sugars until light and fluffy. Beat in the eggs one at a time.

(continued)

3 In a small bowl, sift together the flour, baking powder, and salt. Combine the coffee, milk, and vanilla in another small bowl. Alternately blend the coffee and flour mixtures with the creamed butter. Stir in the walnuts and coconut.

4 Fill the muffin tins and bake until a toothpick inserted in the center of a muffin comes out clean, 25 to 35 minutes. Cool briefly on a wire rack. Serve warm with butter.

· COFFEE AND CREAM WAFFLES ·

L ight and crisp, these waffles deliver a subtle flavor and enticing aroma. A Belgian waffle iron creates a higher waffle than a regular one, but the coffee and cream batter works perfectly in either type of iron.

MAKES 4 TO 6 SERVINGS

3 TABLESPOONS SUGAR

1 ½ CUPS BREWED DARK ROAST
  COFFEE, HOT

1 CUP CREAM

3 EGGS, SEPARATED

4 TABLESPOONS UNSALTED
  BUTTER, MELTED

2 CUPS ALL-PURPOSE FLOUR

1½ TEASPOONS BAKING SODA	UNSALTED BUTTER, MELTED
½ TEASPOON SALT	MAPLE SYRUP
⅛ TEASPOON GROUND	OR
CINNAMON	WHIPPED CREAM

1 Preheat a standard or Belgian waffle iron.

2 In a medium bowl, dissolve the sugar in the hot coffee and allow it to cool slightly. Whisk in the cream, egg yolks, and 4 tablespoons butter.

3 Sift the flour, baking soda, salt, and cinnamon into a medium bowl. Blend the liquid ingredients into the flour mixture. Whisk, if necessary, until the batter is smooth.

4 Beat the egg whites until almost stiff and fold them gently into the batter.

5 Lightly oil the hot waffle iron. Pour about 2 cups of batter onto the iron (depending upon its size), and cook until crisp and golden. Serve immediately with melted butter and maple syrup or whipped cream. Repeat until all the batter is used.

• COFFEE-SCENTED BAKED APPLES •

C offee adds a welcome, if untraditional, flavor and body to these lightly spiced apples. They can be made a day or more ahead and reheated in the microwave for a quick-to-prepare breakfast.

MAKES 4 SERVINGS

4 GRANNY SMITH OR OTHER TART BAKING APPLES

4 TABLESPOONS UNSALTED BUTTER

4 TABLESPOONS LIGHTLY PACKED BROWN SUGAR

1 TEASPOON GROUND CINNAMON

½ CUP BREWED DARK ROAST COFFEE

CREAM (OPTIONAL)

1 Preheat the oven to 350 degrees. Core the apples but do not peel them. Without crowding, place them in a shallow baking dish.

2 Top each apple with 1 tablespoon butter, 1 tablespoon brown sugar, ¼ teaspoon cinnamon, and 2 tablespoons coffee. Bake 45 to 60 minutes, or until the apples are as tender as desired. Baste occasionally during the cooking time.

3 Serve with the cooking liquid warm or cold, with or without cream.

BANANAS BAKED WITH RUM AND COFFEE

B aked bananas make an easy breakfast that can be prepared the night
— before. Increase the sugar to ⅜ cup for a hot dessert to serve over
ice cream.

MAKES 4 SERVINGS

½ CUP BREWED DARK ROAST
  COFFEE
¼ CUP LIGHTLY PACKED BROWN
  SUGAR
4 TABLESPOONS UNSALTED
  BUTTER

2 TABLESPOONS DARK RUM
½ TEASPOON GROUND
  CINNAMON
4 RIPE, FIRM BANANAS,
  PEELED, HALVED LENGTHWISE
CREAM (OPTIONAL)

1 Preheat the oven to 350 degrees. Stir the coffee, sugar, and butter in
a heavy small saucepan over medium heat until the butter melts and
the sugar dissolves.

2 Remove from the heat and blend in the rum and cinnamon. Pour
into a 9-by-13-inch baking dish. Add the bananas to the dish and turn
them once to coat them with the liquid.

3 Bake 10 to 15 minutes, or until the bananas are barely softened.
Broil, if desired, to reduce the liquid. Serve hot with or without cream.

• COFFEE-LACED PRUNES •

C offee adds a deliciously deep and intriguing flavor to an often un-
appreciated fruit. They're a luscious addition to breakfast, over ice
cream for dessert, or packed in a decorative jar to make a tasty gift. If
you're not a prune lover, this recipe will change your mind.

MAKES 1½ CUPS

¼ CUP SUGAR

¾ CUP BREWED DARK ROAST
  COFFEE

1 ½ CUPS PITTED PRUNES

⅓ CUP COFFEE LIQUEUR

2 3-INCH CINNAMON STICKS

ZEST OF ½ LARGE LEMON, CUT
  INTO FINE STRIPS

1 In a heavy small saucepan, stir the sugar and coffee over medium
low heat until the sugar dissolves. Simmer without stirring 5 minutes,
swirling the pan occasionally.

2 Stir in the prunes and simmer uncovered 20 to 30 minutes, or until
the liquid thickens slightly. Add more coffee or water if the liquid reduces
too much.

3 Blend in the coffee liqueur and pour the prunes and cooking liquid
into a clean pint jar. Add the cinnamon sticks and lemon zest. Cover
and chill at least 3 hours before serving. The prunes will keep for up to
two months in the refrigerator.

• APRICOT BREAD ARABICA •

P acked with flavor warm or cold, this easy bread freezes well and
— makes a wonderful gift. The apricots, unlike dates, which are commonly used in quick breads, provide striking contrast in flavor and
color.

MAKES 2 LOAVES

8 OUNCES DRIED APRICOTS,
COARSELY CHOPPED
1¾ CUPS BREWED DARK ROAST
COFFEE, HOT
4 OUNCES UNSALTED BUTTER,
ROOM TEMPERATURE

1½ CUPS SUGAR
2 EGGS
2½ CUPS ALL-PURPOSE FLOUR
2 TEASPOONS BAKING SODA
1 CUP PECANS OR WALNUTS,
COARSELY CHOPPED

1 Combine the apricots and coffee in a small bowl. Cool completely.
Preheat the oven to 350 degrees and grease 2 small loaf pans.

2 In a large bowl, cream the butter with the sugar. Beat in the eggs,
one at a time. Sift the flour with the baking soda, and blend into the
butter alternately with the coffee and apricot mixture. Fold in the
nuts.

3 Divide evenly between the loaf pans, smooth the tops, and bake 1 hour, or until a toothpick inserted in the center comes out clean. Remove from the oven and cool on a wire rack at least 10 minutes. Remove the loaves from the pans and cool completely if not serving immediately.

4 Slice, and serve warm with butter or whipped cream cheese.

• CHESTNUT-HONEY BREAKFAST • SPREAD

P erfect on toast or English muffins, this smooth spread cooks to the consistency and color of apple butter. Roast your own chestnuts during their short season or buy canned nuts for year-round enjoyment and easy preparation.

MAKES 1¼ TO 1½ CUPS

15½ OUNCES CANNED ROASTED
  CHESTNUTS, DRAINED
1½ CUPS MILK
¼ CUP MILD HONEY OR TO
  TASTE

1 TABLESPOON DARK ROAST
  COFFEE BEANS, FINELY
  GROUND
2 TEASPOONS VANILLA
  EXTRACT

1 Coarsely chop the chestnuts and combine them with the milk in a heavy small saucepan.

2 Bring the mixture to a simmer and cook, stirring occasionally, until almost all the liquid evaporates, about 50 minutes. Stir frequently during the last 10 minutes of cooking to prevent scorching.

3 Puree the chestnuts in a food processor or blender. Add the honey, coffee, and vanilla, and puree until completely smooth.

4 Spoon the spread into small jars and seal tightly. Cool, and refrigerate up to a week.

THREE

ENTRÉES

• MAHOGANY-GLAZED CHICKEN •

S erve with fried rice for a delicious hot entrée or use chicken wings
instead of large pieces of meat for an easy hors d'oeuvre. Equally
tasty hot or at room temperature, this richly colored dish also makes
great picnic fare.

MAKES 4 SERVINGS

½ CUP BREWED DARK ROAST
  COFFEE
½ CUP ORANGE JUICE
2 TABLESPOONS MOLASSES
2 TABLESPOONS HONEY

1 TABLESPOON DIJON MUSTARD
3 CLOVES GARLIC, MINCED
1 3½- TO 4-POUND CHICKEN,
  CUT INTO 4 EQUAL PIECES

1 Preheat the oven to 375 degrees. Lightly grease a large baking dish.

2 Blend the coffee, orange juice, molasses, honey, mustard, and garlic
in a medium bowl. Wash the chicken pieces and pat dry.

3 Dip each piece of chicken in the coffee mixture and place in the
baking dish. Pour the remaining liquid over the chicken and bake 45
to 60 minutes, depending upon the thickness of the pieces. Turn them
at least once during cooking.

4 When the chicken juices run clear when the meat is pierced with a sharp knife, remove the chicken from the baking dish and skim off as much fat as possible from the cooking juices. Place the pan over medium-high heat and bring the liquid to a boil, reducing it to a syrupy glaze. Pour over the chicken while hot and serve immediately.

• GINGER-JAVA LAMB KABOBS •

*T*he fresh, zesty tastes of ginger and lemon balance the richness of lamb in these easy-to-prepare kabobs. For added smoked flavor, try throwing ½ pound coffee beans on the hot coals before grilling.

MAKES 4 TO 6 SERVINGS

¾ CUP BREWED DARK ROAST COFFEE, COOLED SLIGHTLY

½ CUP OLIVE OIL

JUICE AND ZEST OF 1 LEMON, MINCED

2 TABLESPOONS MINCED GINGERROOT

2 CLOVES GARLIC, MINCED

½ TEASPOON SALT

1 TEASPOON FRESHLY GROUND PEPPER

1 ½ POUNDS LEG OF LAMB, CUT IN 2-INCH SQUARES

2 RED BELL PEPPERS, CUT IN 2-INCH SQUARES

¼ CUP FRESH CILANTRO LEAVES (OPTIONAL)

1 Blend the coffee, olive oil, lemon juice and zest, gingerroot, garlic, salt, and pepper in a large nonreactive bowl. Add the lamb and bell peppers, tossing to coat evenly. Cover and marinate at room temperature 1 hour or in the refrigerator 4 hours.

2 Preheat a grill or broiler. Skewer the lamb and peppers, alternating meat and vegetables. (If using bamboo skewers, soak them 1 hour in water before grilling to prevent flare-ups.)

3 Grill the kabobs 6 inches from the heat, about 5 minutes on each side for medium rare. Baste at least once while cooking. Place over rice, sprinkle with cilantro, if desired, and drizzle with a little extra marinade. Serve immediately.

· ORANGE AND GARLIC DUCK · BREAST

*T*his dry marinade firms and seasons succulent duck breasts. The combination of pan frying and baking makes the skin crisp, reduces the amount of fat, and keeps the meat rare.

MAKES 4 SERVINGS

2 WHOLE DUCK BREASTS,
  HALVED AND BONED
2 CLOVES GARLIC, MINCED
1 TEASPOON FRESHLY GROUND
  PEPPER
1 TEASPOON GROUND ALLSPICE
1 TEASPOON DRIED THYME
1 TEASPOON SALT
JUICE FROM 2 ORANGES

2 CUPS CHICKEN OR DUCK
  STOCK OR CANNED CHICKEN
  BROTH
1 CUP BREWED DARK ROAST
  COFFEE
2 TABLESPOONS LIGHTLY
  PACKED BROWN SUGAR
½ CUP CREAM
ZEST FROM 2 ORANGES, CUT
  INTO THIN STRIPS

1 Trim any excess fat from the duck breasts, leaving the skin intact. Blend together the garlic, pepper, allspice, thyme, and salt. Rub the meat with the spices and place in a glass baking dish. Cover, chill, and marinate 8 hours or overnight.

2 To cook the duck, remove it from the refrigerator 30 minutes before cooking. Blot off any excess moisture with paper towels. Make 8 or 9 diagonal slices just through the skin of each breast half.

3 Preheat the oven to 350 degrees. Place the duck skin-side down in a heavy large skillet over medium heat. Cook, running a spatula under the breasts occasionally, until they release their fat and the skin is crisp and golden, about 8 minutes.

4 Use 2 tablespoons of the rendered fat to grease a baking dish. Pour off the remaining fat for another use and reserve the skillet. Place the breasts skin-side up on the baking dish and roast 10 to 15 minutes. The duck should register 125 degrees on an instant-read thermometer and should be eaten rare.

5 Meanwhile, place the reserved skillet over high heat and deglaze it with the orange juice and stock or broth, scraping up browned bits clinging to the surface of the pan. Boil vigorously to reduce to a darkened, syrupy glaze.

6 Stir in the coffee, brown sugar, and cream. Lower the heat to medium and reduce again to desired thickness. Stir in the orange zest to warm through. Watch carefully since this mixture can boil over quickly. Remove the duck from the oven and let rest 2 to 3 minutes. Slice following the diagonal slits made before cooking, and serve immediately in a pool of sauce.

• LEMON AND GINGER SHRIMP •

A perfectly balanced blend of spices flavors this quick-to-prepare en-
__ trée. The coffee adds an exotic aroma that complements the lemon
and garlic.

MAKES 4 SERVINGS

4 TABLESPOONS UNSALTED
  BUTTER
4 SHALLOTS, MINCED
½ TEASPOON GROUND GINGER
½ TEASPOON GROUND
  CINNAMON
¼ TEASPOON FRESHLY GROUND
  NUTMEG
2 CLOVES GARLIC, MINCED
1 TABLESPOON MINCED LEMON
  ZEST

¼ CUP FRESH LEMON JUICE
¼ CUP BREWED DARK ROAST
  COFFEE
2 POUNDS FRESH RAW SHRIMP,
  SHELLED AND DEVEINED
1½ TABLESPOONS LIGHTLY
  PACKED BROWN SUGAR
SALT AND FRESHLY GROUND
  PEPPER TO TASTE

1 Melt the butter in a heavy large skillet. Stir in the shallots, ginger, cinnamon, and nutmeg, and cook over medium-low heat until the shallots soften, about 5 minutes.

2 Add the garlic, lemon zest, lemon juice, coffee, and shrimp. Increase the heat and sauté until the shrimp are barely cooked. If the liquid is not reduced to 1 to 2 tablespoons, remove the shrimp and cook the liquid down.

3 Return the shrimp to the pan, if necessary, and toss them with the brown sugar until the sugar melts and glazes the shrimp. Add salt and pepper to taste. Serve immediately.

GLAZED CHICKEN WITH SAUTÉED APPLES

C offee provides the robust flavor and deep-brown color in this un-
usually delicious entrée. Buy chicken breasts already boned and skinned, so that the entire dish can be made in 15 minutes flat.

MAKES 4 SERVINGS

4 TABLESPOONS UNSALTED BUTTER

4 LARGE CHICKEN BREAST HALVES, BONED AND SKINNED

4 TEASPOONS LIGHTLY PACKED BROWN SUGAR

2 TABLESPOONS COFFEE LIQUEUR

¼ CUP BREWED DARK ROAST COFFEE

¼ CUP APPLE CIDER OR ORANGE JUICE

1 LARGE GRANNY SMITH APPLE, PEELED, CORED, AND CUT INTO ¼-INCH WEDGES

SALT AND FRESHLY GROUND PEPPER TO TASTE

1 Melt 3 tablespoons of the butter in a heavy large skillet over medium-high heat. Without crowding, brown the chicken in the butter, turning once. Sprinkle 1 teaspoon brown sugar over each breast half and turn once more. Continue cooking until the sugar melts, about one minute.

2 Remove the chicken to a warm plate and cover loosely with foil to keep it warm. Over medium-high heat, deglaze the pan with the coffee liqueur, scraping up any browned bits on the bottom. Whisk in the coffee and apple cider or orange juice and reduce until slightly thickened, about 3 minutes.

3 In a separate pan, melt the remaining tablespoon of butter over medium-high heat. Add the apple wedges and sauté, turning as needed, until golden on both sides.

4 Return the chicken breasts to the original pan, cover partially, and simmer until the chicken is finished cooking. It should be springy to the touch. Turn the chicken at least once in the coffee glaze. Taste, and adjust the seasoning with salt and pepper.

5 To serve, place a breast half on each plate and top with sautéed apple wedges. Spoon any remaining glaze over the apples and serve immediately.

FOUR

SIDE DISHES

• COFFEE-RYE BREAD •

C offee adds a pleasing aroma to this light, moist rye bread.

MAKES 2 ROUND LOAVES

4 TO 4½ CUPS ALL-PURPOSE
  FLOUR (APPROXIMATE)
2 CUPS DARK RYE FLOUR
¼ CUP UNSWEETENED COCOA
  POWDER
2 TO 3 TABLESPOONS CARAWAY
  SEEDS
2 TABLESPOONS ACTIVE DRY
  YEAST

2 TEASPOONS SALT
2 CUPS BREWED DARK ROAST
  COFFEE
⅓ CUP MOLASSES
2 TABLESPOONS UNSALTED
  BUTTER, MELTED
CORNMEAL

1 Place 2 cups of the all-purpose flour, the rye flour, cocoa, caraway, yeast, and salt in the bowl of a heavy-duty mixer.

2 Blend the coffee, molasses, and butter in a heavy small saucepan. Heat to 115 degrees. Using the dough hook with the mixer on medium-low speed, gradually pour in the liquid. When well incorporated, add the remaining flour, a little at a time, until the dough pulls away from the sides of the bowl. Knead at medium speed until the dough feels firm and elastic. (If using a lightweight mixer, remove the dough from the bowl after incorporating the liquid, and add the flour, kneading by hand until it is smooth and elastic.)

3 Place in an oiled bowl, cover, and let rise in a warm place until doubled, 45 minutes to 1 hour. Punch down and knead briefly. Divide evenly and shape into 2 round loaves. Place on a greased baking sheet sprinkled with cornmeal. Cover lightly and let rise in a warm place until almost doubled, 30 to 45 minutes.

4 Preheat the oven to 375 degrees. Make deep slashes through the tops of the loaves with a sharp knife or razor blade. Bake 35 to 40 minutes or until the loaves sound hollow when lightly tapped.

5 Remove the loaves to a wire rack to cool. Slice and serve warm with butter.

• ONION-COFFEE CONFIT •

C onfit is a food preserved and tenderized by slow cooking. It is commonly associated with duck and goose, but vegetable counterparts make interesting fare. Serve this coffee-enriched confit at room temperature with paté or warm with poultry, pork, or game. Use frozen pearl onions if fresh are not available.

MAKES ABOUT 2½ CUPS

1 POUND (ABOUT 60) PEARL
ONIONS, TRIMMED AND
PEELED (SEE NOTE)
1 ¼ CUPS BREWED DARK ROAST
COFFEE
¼ CUP BALSAMIC OR RED WINE
VINEGAR

¼ CUP SUGAR
2 TABLESPOONS OLIVE OIL
3 TABLESPOONS TOMATO
PASTE
½ CUP RAISINS

1 Place all the ingredients in a heavy medium saucepan. Bring to a boil, reduce the heat, and simmer partly covered 40 minutes or until the onions are tender.

2 Watch carefully, and add more coffee or water if too much liquid evaporates. The liquid should thicken and reduce to the consistency of chutney.

NOTE: *TO TRIM AND PEEL PEARL ONIONS,* bring a large amount of water to boil in a heavy saucepan. Blanch the onions about 15 seconds. Drain and rinse them with cold water until they are cool to the touch. Trim the stem and root ends, and slip the skins off with your fingers.

• COFFEE-GLAZED CARROTS •

*T*he orange juice and liqueur heighten the natural sweetness of carrots in this easy dish. It makes a convenient and colorful do-ahead vegetable for company—just reheat in the microwave when ready to serve.

MAKES 6 SERVINGS

8 MEDIUM CARROTS, PEELED
  AND TRIMMED
1 CUP ORANGE JUICE
2 TABLESPOONS UNSALTED
  BUTTER

⅜ CUP COFFEE LIQUEUR
⅛ TEASPOON GROUND
  CINNAMON
SALT AND FRESHLY GROUND
  PEPPER TO TASTE

1 Cut the carrots on the diagonal in ¼-inch slices. Place in a heavy medium saucepan with the orange juice, butter, ¼ cup of the liqueur, and cinnamon.

(continued)

2 Bring the mixture to a boil, reduce the heat, and simmer uncovered, stirring occasionally, until all the liquid is absorbed, about 15 minutes.

3 Stir in the remaining 2 tablespoons liqueur. Cook the carrots several minutes more, shaking the pan frequently until they take on a glaze. Season with salt and pepper and serve immediately.

· BOSTON BROWN BREAD ·

T his batter can be steamed in an ordinary metal bowl to produce a round loaf or in a metal can for a cylindrical one. Traditionally served with molasses-flavored baked beans or a boiled dinner, it's also a satisfying breakfast bread.

MAKES 1 LOAF, 10 TO 12 SERVINGS

½ CUP BREWED DARK ROAST
  COFFEE, HOT
½ CUP RAISINS
⅝ CUP WHOLE WHEAT OR
  GRAHAM FLOUR
½ CUP ALL-PURPOSE FLOUR

½ CUP CORNMEAL
½ TEASPOON SALT
½ TEASPOON BAKING SODA
½ TEASPOON BAKING POWDER
½ CUP BUTTERMILK
½ CUP MOLASSES

1 Bring a large kettle of water to a simmer. Combine the coffee and raisins in a small bowl, and allow to cool slightly.

2 Combine the flours, cornmeal, salt, baking soda, and baking powder in a medium bowl. Blend the buttermilk and molasses together, and stir into the cooled raisins and coffee. Combine the liquid ingredients with the dry, stirring until just blended.

3 Pour the batter into a 6-cup metal can or bowl, cover with foil, and place in the kettle with simmering water at least halfway up the can. Cover the kettle, and steam 2 hours, 10 minutes. Check the level of water occasionally, since it may need replenishing.

4 Remove the loaf from the kettle and place on a wire rack to cool at least 10 minutes. Run a narrow spatula around the inside of the container and remove the bread. Slice and serve warm with butter or whipped cream cheese.

WINTER SQUASH BAKED WITH COFFEE LIQUEUR

*A*corn squash make attractive serving containers as well as nutritious, — easy-to-prepare vegetables. Winter squash are bargains during their fall season, and coffee liqueur gives them depth of color and richness in flavor.

MAKES 4 SERVINGS

2 MEDIUM ACORN SQUASH

4 TABLESPOONS UNSALTED
  BUTTER, MELTED

¼ CUP COFFEE LIQUEUR

¼ TEASPOON FRESHLY GRATED
  NUTMEG

SALT AND FRESHLY GROUND
  PEPPER TO TASTE

1 Preheat the oven to 350 degrees. Slice the squash in half lengthwise and scoop out the seeds. Cut a small slice off the bottom of each half, if necessary, to make it sit flat. Place skin-side down in a shallow baking dish.

2 In a small bowl, combine the butter, liqueur, and nutmeg. Divide the mixture evenly among the squash halves and bake, basting occasionally, for 1 hour. Season with salt and pepper and serve immediately.

FIVE

SAUCES

• BLUEBERRY-PORT SAUCE •

E qually delicious with poultry or pork, this sweet-sour sauce provides
maximum flavor with minimum effort.

MAKES 2 TO 2½ CUPS

1 CUP CHICKEN STOCK OR
  CANNED CHICKEN BROTH
½ CUP BREWED DARK ROAST
  COFFEE
½ CUP FRESH OR FROZEN
  BLUEBERRIES
¼ CUP PORT
2 TABLESPOONS SUGAR

2 TO 3 TEASPOONS BLUEBERRY
  OR RASPBERRY VINEGAR
1 TABLESPOON CORNSTARCH
  DISSOLVED IN 1 TABLESPOON
  WATER
SALT AND FRESHLY GROUND
  PEPPER TO TASTE

1 Combine the stock or broth, coffee, blueberries, port, and sugar in a
heavy small saucepan. Stir over medium-high heat until the sugar dissolves.

2 Blend in the vinegar, bring to a boil, reduce the heat, and simmer
10 minutes. Blend the cornstarch and water in a small bowl, and stir it
into the sauce. Continue to simmer, stirring, for one minute. Taste and
adjust the seasoning, if needed, with salt and freshly ground pepper.
Serve while warm.

• COFFEE-NUTMEG SYRUP •

P our this fragrant syrup over pancakes or waffles for a special breakfast. It's fast and simple to make, and packed into a decorative jar with a vanilla bean, the syrup makes a unique gift.

MAKES ABOUT 2½ CUPS

2 CUPS BREWED DARK ROAST
  COFFEE

1 CUP SUGAR

2 TABLESPOONS ALL-PURPOSE
  FLOUR

½ TEASPOON FRESHLY GRATED
  NUTMEG

2 TABLESPOONS UNSALTED
  BUTTER

1 TEASPOON VANILLA EXTRACT

1 Whisk the coffee, sugar, flour, and nutmeg in a heavy medium saucepan until smooth. Stir over medium heat until the mixture comes to a boil. Reduce the heat and simmer 3 minutes.

2 Remove the pan from the heat and whisk in the butter until it melts completely. Stir in the vanilla and serve warm over pancakes or waffles.

• COFFEE-TOFFEE SAUCE •

*T*his warm toffee sauce cools down to a luscious, deep caramel-colored syrup. Try it over pancakes for a lavish breakfast. It keeps a week covered and chilled.

MAKES ABOUT 1 CUP

1 CUP LIGHTLY PACKED BROWN
  SUGAR
½ CUP BREWED DARK ROAST
  COFFEE

1 EGG
1 TO 2 TABLESPOONS COFFEE
  LIQUEUR (OPTIONAL)

1 In a heavy small saucepan over medium heat, stir the sugar and coffee until the sugar dissolves. Bring to a boil, reduce the heat, and simmer 5 minutes.

2 Beat the egg in a medium bowl. While whisking, slowly drizzle in the coffee and sugar. Return the mixture to the heat and whisk for another 2 minutes. Do not allow it to boil. The sauce should be very thick. Remove from the heat and strain if not perfectly smooth.

3 Blend in the liqueur, if desired, and serve warm or cold over ice cream, poached pears, or baked apples.

VARIATIONS:

HAZELNUT-COFFEE-TOFFEE SAUCE: Substitute Frangelico for the coffee liqueur. Add ¼ cup coarsely chopped hazelnuts, toasted and skinned, just before serving.

BRANDIED-COFFEE-TOFFEE SAUCE: Substitute 1 tablespoon brandy for the coffee liqueur.

ORANGE-COFFEE-TOFFEE SAUCE: Substitute orange liqueur for the coffee liqueur, and stir in 2 teaspoons finely grated orange zest just before serving.

• MOCHA SAUCE •

D ivinely chocolate, rich, and decadent, this sauce is irresistible. Serve it warm over ice cream or pour it into the blender with milk and ice cream for a great shake.

MAKES ABOUT 1 CUP

4 OUNCES BEST-QUALITY SEMI-
SWEET CHOCOLATE, GRATED
¼ CUP BREWED ESPRESSO OR
DOUBLE-STRENGTH DARK
ROAST COFFEE

2 TABLESPOONS UNSALTED
BUTTER
2 TABLESPOONS CREAM
2 TABLESPOONS COFFEE
LIQUEUR

1 Stir the chocolate, espresso, butter, and cream in a heavy small saucepan over medium-low heat. When the chocolate melts and the mixture is completely smooth, remove it from the heat and whisk in the liqueur.

2 Serve warm or at room temperature. If not using immediately, store airtight in the refrigerator for up to 2 weeks. Reheat gently to serve.

• COFFEE-CHANTILLY SAUCE •

D elicate coffee and vanilla flavors highlight this sauce. Using real
— vanilla bean transforms the recipe from a pleasure to an indulgence.
Add freshly grated nutmeg or cinnamon for a fragrant variation.

MAKES 1¼ TO 1½ CUPS

2 EGGS

½ CUP BREWED DARK ROAST
  COFFEE, COOLED SLIGHTLY

¼ CUP SUGAR

1 VANILLA BEAN, SPLIT
  LENGTHWISE, OR 1 TEASPOON
  VANILLA EXTRACT

¼ CUP CREAM, WHIPPED TO
  SOFT PEAKS

1 Beat the eggs in the top of a double boiler off the heat. Whisk in the
coffee and sugar. Place over simmering water, add the vanilla bean, if
using, and stir until the sauce coats the back of a spoon. Remove from
the heat, pour into a medium bowl, cover, and chill.

2 Remove the vanilla bean and scrape out the tiny seeds. If the sauce
is not completely smooth at this point, strain it into another bowl. Whisk
the vanilla seeds into the sauce or stir in the vanilla extract, if using.
Just before serving, fold in the whipped cream.

· HOT FUDGE SAUCE ·

*T*his sumptuous, candy-like sauce of dark chocolate has a haunting aroma of coffee that's perfect over vanilla ice cream. The coffee-flavored sugar syrup reduces and concentrates as it reaches the soft-ball stage, so it's thick enough to set on contact with a cold dessert.

MAKES ABOUT 1¾ CUPS

5 OUNCES DARK UNSWEETENED CHOCOLATE, GRATED
2 TABLESPOONS UNSALTED BUTTER
¾ CUP BREWED DARK ROAST COFFEE

¾ CUP SUGAR
1½ TABLESPOONS LIGHT CORN SYRUP
3 TABLESPOONS MILK

1 Melt the chocolate and butter in the top of a double boiler over simmering water.

2 Meanwhile, stir the coffee, sugar, and corn syrup in a heavy medium saucepan over medium heat until the sugar dissolves. Cook without stirring until it reads 234 degrees on a candy thermometer.

3 Stir the coffee mixture into the melted chocolate and butter. Whisk in the milk vigorously, and keep warm until ready to serve. If not using immediately, cool the sauce and keep it refrigerated up to 1 month. When ready to use, reheat it gently, and whisk before serving.

SIX

DESSERTS

• TIRAMISÙ •

*T*his silken, not-too-sweet dessert highlights many trendy restaurant menus today. Italians often make Tiramisù with leftover cake or panettone, but ladyfingers, whether homemade or store-bought, lend the dessert a distinctive look. The name means "pick-me-up," which refers to the caffeine in the espresso.

MAKES 8 TO 12 SERVINGS

LADYFINGERS

4 EGGS, SEPARATED

½ CUP SUGAR

½ TEASPOON VANILLA EXTRACT

1 CUP ALL-PURPOSE FLOUR, SIFTED

2 TABLESPOONS POWDERED SUGAR

⅜ CUP BREWED ESPRESSO OR DOUBLE-STRENGTH DARK ROAST COFFEE, COOLED SLIGHTLY

2 TABLESPOONS COFFEE LIQUEUR

FILLING

5 EGGS, SEPARATED

½ CUP SUGAR

1 POUND MASCARPONE OR CREAM CHEESE, ROOM TEMPERATURE

⅝ CUP HEAVY CREAM

⅜ CUP COFFEE LIQUEUR

3 OUNCES SEMISWEET CHOCOLATE, GRATED

1 To make the ladyfingers, preheat the oven to 350 degrees. Line a large baking sheet with parchment paper or foil. Grease it lightly.

2 In a medium bowl, beat the egg yolks, sugar, and vanilla until thick and fluffy. Sprinkle the flour over the yolks and fold in gently. Whip the egg whites to soft peaks. While beating, add 2 tablespoons powdered sugar gradually. Continue to beat to almost stiff peaks. Fold the whites into the flour mixture gently.

3 Pipe the batter onto the prepared baking sheet in 3-by-1-inch strips, about 1 inch apart. Bake 10 to 12 minutes, or until the ladyfingers are golden. When cool enough to handle, transfer them to a wire rack to cool completely.

4 Blend the espresso and 2 tablespoons of the coffee liqueur in a small bowl. Brush lightly onto the ladyfingers. Line the bottom and sides of a 3-quart glass bowl or two large loaf pans with three-quarters of the ladyfingers, trimming them so they do not overlap.

5 To make the filling, in a large bowl, beat the egg yolks and sugar until thickened, pale, and fluffy. Beat in the mascarpone or cream cheese. When smooth, beat in the cream and the remaining ⅜ cup liqueur. In a separate bowl, beat the egg whites to almost stiff peaks. Fold them into the mascarpone mixture.

(continued)

6 Spread half the mascarpone over the ladyfingers and sprinkle with half the grated chocolate. Arrange the remaining ladyfingers over the chocolate, trimming as needed. Pour the remaining mascarpone over the ladyfingers and decorate with the remaining chocolate. Cover and chill at least 8 hours before spooning into individual serving dishes.

· CRÈME CARAMEL CAFÉ ·

*U*ltra smooth and satiny, this custard blends two favorite flavors, caramel and coffee, to make a luxurious, untraditional combination.

MAKES 8 SERVINGS

½ CUP SUGAR

1 ⅓ CUPS CREAM
⅔ CUP MILK
2½ TABLESPOONS DARK ROAST
  COFFEE BEANS, FINELY
  GROUND

6 EGGS, ROOM TEMPERATURE
⅜ CUP SUGAR
3 TABLESPOONS COFFEE
  LIQUEUR
2 TEASPOONS VANILLA
  EXTRACT

1 Heat ½ cup sugar with 2 tablespoons water in a heavy small saucepan over medium-high heat. Cook without stirring until the sugar darkens slightly. Swirl the pan once and continue to cook without stirring until the sugar caramelizes into a light-brown syrup.

2 Vigorously whisk in 2 more tablespoons water, being careful of splattering. Remove from the heat and immediately pour into 8 custard cups. Swirl the mixture quickly around the bottom and sides of each cup.

3 Preheat the oven to 325 degrees. Stir the cream, milk, and ground coffee in a heavy medium saucepan. Bring to a simmer, remove from the heat, cover, and let steep 15 minutes. Strain the mixture into a clean saucepan and reheat to a simmer.

4 Meanwhile, beat the eggs and sugar until thickened. While whisking, drizzle in the hot cream mixture. Return it to the pan and stir constantly over low heat until the custard thickens slightly, about 5 minutes. Do not allow it to boil.

5 Blend in the liqueur and vanilla. Pour into the custard cups. Place the cups in a large baking pan and fill the pan carefully with boiling water to come two-thirds up the sides of the cups.

6 Bake 25 minutes. The custards will still look wobbly in the center. Remove from the water bath, allow to cool to room temperature, and chill at least 2 hours.

7 To serve, run a knife around the inside of each custard cup. Place the bottom of each cup in hot water for 5 seconds, place a serving plate on top of each and invert.

. CHILLED ESPRESSO .
ZABAGLIONE

S pecial copper pans with wooden handles and rounded shapes are
— designed to create ethereal zabaglione. The metal transfers heat
quickly, the shape allows a wire whisk to reach every bit of yolk, and
the wooden handle provides easy control of the bowl. This cooled version, unlike the traditional warm one, can be made hours ahead.

MAKES 6 SERVINGS

6 EGG YOLKS

1 CUP SUGAR

¾ CUP BREWED ESPRESSO,
 ROOM TEMPERATURE

2 TABLESPOONS COFFEE
 LIQUEUR

1 CUP CREAM

6 STRIPS LEMON ZEST
 (OPTIONAL)

1 In a large metal bowl with a smooth rounded shape, whisk the egg
yolks with the sugar until thick and light.

2 Blend in the espresso and liqueur, and place the bowl at least 3 inches
over simmering water. Whisk constantly until the mixture expands and
lightens, about 10 minutes.

3 When the zabaglione foams and thickens, remove the metal bowl from the heat to a larger bowl filled with ice water. Continue whisking until the mixture is cool to the touch.

4 Whip the cream to soft peaks. Fold the cream into the zabaglione and pour into 6 wineglasses. Serve immediately with a strip of lemon zest, if desired, or cover and keep chilled up to 6 hours.

• MOCHA MOUSSE •

U nsweetened cocoa powder delivers delicate chocolate flavor without adding heaviness to this airy dessert. The nuts provide interesting texture, but they can be eliminated if a smooth mousse is preferred.

MAKES 6 SERVINGS

1 ENVELOPE UNFLAVORED
GELATIN

1 CUP BREWED DARK ROAST
COFFEE, ROOM TEMPERATURE

1 CUP SUGAR

3 TABLESPOONS UNSWEET-
ENED COCOA POWDER

3 EGGS, SEPARATED

1 TEASPOON VANILLA EXTRACT

¾ CUP COARSELY CHOPPED
MACADAMIA NUTS, LIGHTLY
TOASTED (OPTIONAL)

¾ CUP CREAM

WHIPPED CREAM (OPTIONAL)

COCOA POWDER (OPTIONAL)

1 Stir the gelatin into ¼ cup of the coffee in a small bowl. Let soften at least 5 minutes.

2 Blend the remaining ¾ cup coffee, the sugar, and the cocoa powder in a heavy small saucepan. Stir constantly over medium heat to dissolve the sugar and cocoa.

3 Whisk the egg yolks in a medium bowl until lightened. While whisking, drizzle in the hot cocoa mixture. Return the mixture to the saucepan over low heat and stir constantly for 5 minutes. Do not allow it to boil.

4 Remove the mixture from the heat and whisk in the softened gelatin. When the gelatin dissolves, remove it to a large bowl and stir in the vanilla extract. Cover and chill until it mounds slightly when dropped from a spoon (or place the bowl directly over a larger bowl of ice water and whisk occasionally to hasten the chilling).

5 Stir in the chopped nuts, if using. Whip the cream to soft peaks and fold it into the chocolate. Beat the egg whites to soft peaks. Fold a third of the whites into the chocolate, then fold in the remaining whites.

6 Pour into 6 chilled stemmed glasses, cover, and chill at least 3 hours before serving. Top with extra whipped cream dusted with cocoa powder, if desired.

• BLACK RUSSIAN MOUSSE •

*N*amed for the well-known Black Russian cocktail made with Kahlúa and vodka, this unusual mousse is airy in texture, but most full in flavor. It can easily be made a day or two ahead. Accompany this dessert with a crisp cookie or a few strawberries for contrast.

MAKES 6 SERVINGS

1 ENVELOPE UNFLAVORED
  GELATIN
⅓ CUP COFFEE LIQUEUR
½ CUP BREWED DARK ROAST
  COFFEE, HOT

2 EGGS, SEPARATED
½ CUP SUGAR
⅓ CUP VODKA
1½ CUPS CREAM

1 In an small bowl, blend the gelatin with the coffee liqueur and let it soften 5 minutes. Whisk the gelatin mixture into the hot coffee to dissolve it completely. Cool slightly.

2 In a large bowl, whisk the egg yolks and sugar until light and thick. Blend in the vodka and the coffee mixture. Cover and chill, stirring occasionally, until slightly thickened, about 45 minutes. (Or place over a larger bowl of ice water and whisk occasionally until slightly thickened.) Whisk thoroughly, so the mixture is completely smooth.

3 Whip the cream until soft peaks form and fold it into the coffee mixture. In a separate bowl, beat the egg whites to almost stiff peaks. Gently fold them into the mousse. Pour into 6 coffee cups or stemmed wineglasses, cover, and chill at least 3 hours.

• COFFEE BREAD PUDDING •

*A*s this unusual dessert cooks, the brown sugar melts, forming a sauce that coats the top of the unmolded pudding. The coffee adds a fresh dimension to this old-fashioned comfort food.

MAKES 6 SERVINGS

2 CUPS MILK

⅓ CUP DARK ROAST COFFEE BEANS, GROUND TO A MEDIUM COARSENESS

1 CUP LIGHTLY PACKED BROWN SUGAR, FREE OF LUMPS

2 TABLESPOONS UNSALTED BUTTER, SOFTENED

3 SLICES BREAD

1 CUP RAISINS OR DRIED CURRANTS

3 EGGS

1 TEASPOON VANILLA EXTRACT

DASH OF SALT

1 Stir the milk and coffee in a heavy small saucepan. Bring to a boil, reduce the heat, and simmer one minute. Remove from the heat and stir. Cover, and let steep 15 minutes.

2 Meanwhile, place the sugar in the top of a double boiler, packing it down lightly and evenly. Spread the butter over the slices of bread, dice them into ½-inch cubes, and sprinkle the cubes over the sugar. Sprinkle the raisins or currants over the bread.

3 Strain the milk into a clean bowl and discard the grounds. Beat the eggs in a medium bowl. While whisking, drizzle the milk into the eggs. Blend in the vanilla and salt.

4 Pour the liquid over the bread but do *not* stir. Place over simmering water, cover, and cook for one hour. Remove the top of the double boiler from the water and let rest 10 minutes.

5 To serve, uncover, run a knife around the inside edge of the boiler, and invert the pudding onto a serving dish. Slice into 6 wedges and serve with the sauce the brown sugar forms as the pudding cooks.

• MOCHA POTS DE CRÈME •

S ince this intensely flavored chocolate dessert is exceptionally rich, serve it in demitasses or tiny dishes for which the dessert was named. A pot de crème is a small ceramic dish with a lid used for individual hot and cold desserts.

MAKES 8 SERVINGS

8 OUNCES GOOD-QUALITY SEMI-
SWEET CHOCOLATE, GRATED
5 TABLESPOONS BREWED
ESPRESSO OR DOUBLE-
STRENGTH DARK ROAST
COFFEE
5 EGGS, SEPARATED

3 TABLESPOONS COFFEE
LIQUEUR
½ CUP CREAM
1 TABLESPOON SUGAR
8 CHOCOLATE-COVERED
ESPRESSO BEANS (OPTIONAL)

1 In a heavy small saucepan, gently melt the chocolate with the espresso, stirring over low heat. Remove it from the heat and scrape the chocolate into a medium bowl. Whisk in the egg yolks, one at a time. Beat in 2 tablespoons of the liqueur.

2 In a separate bowl, beat the egg whites until they hold soft peaks. Fold them gently into the chocolate mixture. Pour into 8 small coffee cups, cover, and chill at least 6 hours.

3 Just before serving, whip the cream in a chilled bowl until thickened. Continue beating while adding the sugar and the remaining 1 tablespoon liqueur. Beat until the cream is stiff.

4 To serve, uncover the pot de crème and top each with about 2 tablespoons of the whipped cream. Top the whipped cream with a chocolate-covered espresso bean, if desired.

• MAPLE CRÈME BRÛLÉE CAFÉ •

T his dessert is intended for serious dark roast fans only. For a more subtle flavor, substitute a medium roast bean. The crisp caramel topping is the perfect counterpoint to a moist, perfectly smooth, coffee-infused cream.

MAKES 8 SERVINGS

2 CUPS CREAM

½ CUP DARK ROAST COFFEE
   BEANS, FINELY GROUND

1 CUP MAPLE SYRUP

6 EGG YOLKS

½ CUP SUGAR

1 Preheat the oven to 325 degrees.

2 In a heavy medium saucepan, blend the cream and coffee and bring it to a simmer, stirring occasionally. Cover, remove from the heat, and let steep 15 minutes. Strain the cream into a clean saucepan and stir in the maple syrup. Reheat, stirring occasionally, until the liquid simmers.

3 Whisk the egg yolks in a large bowl. While whisking, drizzle in a cup of the hot cream. Pour in the remaining cream while continuing to whisk. Strain the mixture into 8 ½-cup ramekins.

4 Place the ramekins in a large baking pan. Fill the pan carefully with boiling water to come halfway up the sides of the dishes. Carefully place in the oven and bake 25 to 30 minutes or until barely set. Remove from the water bath, cover loosely, and chill at least 4 hours.

5 Preheat the broiler 10 minutes. Uncover the ramekins and dab with paper toweling if moist on top. Sprinkle the sugar evenly over the custards and broil close to the flame, watching closely, until the sugar browns and melts, 2 to 3 minutes. Cool, and serve within 2 to 3 hours so the topping remains crisp.

MOCHA FONDUE WITH STRAWBERRIES

T his simple but elegant dessert can be fixed in a flash. If strawberries
—— aren't available, use 1-inch chunks of banana, orange sections, biscotti, or bite-size pieces of angel food or pound cake for dipping.

MAKES 6 SERVINGS

18 OUNCES GOOD-QUALITY
SEMISWEET OR DARK
CHOCOLATE, GRATED
½ CUP BREWED ESPRESSO OR
DOUBLE-STRENGTH DARK
ROAST COFFEE

¼ CUP CREAM
6 TABLESPOONS COFFEE
LIQUEUR
30 PERFECT RIPE STRAWBER-
RIES

1 Place the chocolate, espresso, and cream in the top of a double boiler
over simmering water. Stir occasionally until the chocolate melts. Add
the liqueur and whisk until the mixture is smooth and warm.

2 Pour equal portions into stemmed sherbert or wide-mouth wineglasses. Place each glass on a plate and surround with 5 perfect strawberries. Serve immediately after pouring, so the fondue stays warm.

SEVEN

CANDIES AND COOKIES

• ALMOND-COFFEE TOFFEE •

*S*ince this rich toffee keeps for months, it makes an easy do-ahead gift for coffee fans. The recipe can be doubled or tripled easily, but be sure to use a large enough pan to allow the sugar syrup to foam. It's best to have nuts warm when incorporating them into toffee—otherwise, they cool down the candy so quickly, it becomes difficult to pour.

MAKES ABOUT 4 POUNDS

6 OUNCES UNSALTED
  BLANCHED ALMONDS,
  COARSELY CHOPPED
1 CUP UNSALTED BUTTER
1½ CUPS SUGAR
¼ CUP BREWED DARK ROAST
  COFFEE

1 TABLESPOON LIGHT CORN
  SYRUP
¼ CUP DARK ROAST BEANS,
  COARSELY CHOPPED
24 OUNCES SEMISWEET
  CHOCOLATE, GRATED

1 Preheat the oven to 350 degrees. Line a 9-by-13-inch baking sheet with foil or parchment paper. Butter the liner.

2 Spread the almonds evenly over a second baking sheet and toast them until lightly browned, 10 to 12 minutes. Remove from the oven and reserve.

3 Stir the butter, sugar, coffee, and corn syrup in a heavy, deep saucepan over medium heat until the butter melts and the sugar dissolves. Bring to a boil and simmer without stirring until the mixture reaches 300 degrees on a candy thermometer.

4 Quickly stir in the almonds and coffee beans. Pour immediately onto the buttered baking sheet and cool completely.

5 Melt the chocolate gently in the top of a double boiler or in the microwave. Spread half of the chocolate evenly over one side of the toffee. When the chocolate has set, invert the sheet of toffee onto waxed paper or foil and remove the liner. Spread the remaining chocolate over the inverted toffee.

6 When the chocolate has set, break the toffee into small irregular pieces. Store airtight.

CHOCOLATE-ESPRESSO TRUFFLES

C offee heightens the flavor of chocolate in these rich, melt-in-your-mouth morsels. The truffles will keep a few days chilled or a month frozen.

MAKES 18 LARGE TRUFFLES

¾ CUP CREAM

3 TABLESPOONS DARK ROAST COFFEE BEANS, FINELY GROUND

8 OUNCES GOOD-QUALITY SEMI-SWEET CHOCOLATE, CHOPPED

4 TABLESPOONS UNSALTED BUTTER, ROOM TEMPERATURE

1 TABLESPOON COFFEE LIQUEUR

¼ CUP COCOA POWDER

1 Stir the cream and coffee over medium-low heat in a heavy small saucepan. Bring to a simmer while stirring. Remove from the heat, cover, and let steep 15 minutes.

2 Strain the mixture and return it to a clean pan. Reheat slowly to a simmer, remove from the heat, and whisk in the chocolate and butter. Continue whisking until the mixture is completely smooth.

3 Blend in the liqueur. Transfer to a bowl, cover, and chill at least 4 hours.

4 Roll into roughly shaped, quarter-sized balls. Just before serving, roll in cocoa powder, shaking off any excess. Keep covered and chilled, since the truffles soften quickly at room temperature.

• TROPICAL TRUFFLES •

T he sweet buttery quality of white chocolate complements the acidity in coffee beans beautifully. These truffles freeze well, so keep some on hand for emergencies. Be sure to stir the coconut milk before using, since it separates in the can.

MAKES 50

10 OUNCES WHITE CHOCOLATE, GRATED

3 TABLESPOONS CANNED COCONUT MILK

3 TABLESPOONS CREAM

1⅓ CUPS FINELY GRATED SWEETENED COCONUT

50 COFFEE BEANS

1 In a heavy small saucepan, melt the chocolate with the coconut milk and cream, stirring frequently. When smooth, blend in ⅓ cup of the grated coconut. Cover and chill 8 hours or until moldable.

2 Wrap a small amount of the chocolate mixture around each espresso bean, shaping into rough circles. If the mixture becomes too warm to work with, rechill 10 to 15 minutes.

3 While the truffles are warm from being shaped, roll each in the remaining cup of coconut. Chill or freeze until ready to serve.

• MALABAR MACAROONS •

T hese light, chewy, unorthodox morsels are for serious coffee fans. Alter the amount of coffee flavor, if you like, by choosing a light roast coffee bean or by changing the proportion of pecans to beans. Just be sure to include a total of 1 cup beans and nuts. The food processor makes these a breeze to prepare.

MAKES 20

¾ CUP PECANS

¼ CUP COFFEE BEANS

10 TABLESPOONS SUGAR

1 EGG WHITE

2 TABLESPOONS LIGHTLY
  PACKED BROWN SUGAR

20 PECAN HALVES

1 Preheat the oven to 325 degrees and position a rack in the upper third of the oven. Line a baking sheet with waxed paper or parchment. Lightly butter the paper.

2 Place the pecans, coffee beans, and 2 tablespoons of the sugar in the bowl of a food processor. Grind the nuts and beans until they are chopped to a powder.

3 Add the egg white and process 10 seconds. Add the remaining 8 tablespoons (½ cup) sugar and process about 15 seconds, scraping down the sides of the bowl, if needed. Add the brown sugar and mix 10 seconds more.

4 Dampen your palms with water. Roll 2 teaspoons of the batter at a time between them, squeezing the mixture lightly, if needed, to prevent crumbling. Place on the prepared baking sheet. Repeat, spacing the macaroons about 1 inch apart, until all the mixture is used.

5 Press 1 pecan half into the center of each cookie. Bake 20 minutes and remove the baking sheet from the oven. With a metal spatula, remove each cookie to a wire rack to cool completely. Store airtight for up to a week.

· FROSTED ESPRESSO BROWNIES ·

*T*he aroma of dark roast coffee transforms this basic but rich brownie into an adult indulgence. For a lighter, cakier brownie, use 3 ounces chocolate instead of 6 and reduce the baking time by 5 to 10 minutes. If you can save any, freeze them for up to 2 months.

MAKES 16

BROWNIES

½ CUP UNSALTED BUTTER

6 OUNCES SEMISWEET
  CHOCOLATE, GRATED

¼ CUP ESPRESSO OR DOUBLE-
  STRENGTH DARK ROAST
  COFFEE

2 EGGS

¾ CUP SUGAR

2 TEASPOONS VANILLA
  EXTRACT

¾ CUP ALL-PURPOSE FLOUR

1 CUP COARSELY CHOPPED
  PECANS OR WALNUTS
  (OPTIONAL)

FROSTING

1 OUNCE SEMISWEET
  CHOCOLATE, GRATED

1 TABLESPOON UNSALTED
  BUTTER

1½ TABLESPOONS ESPRESSO
  OR DOUBLE-STRENGTH DARK
  ROAST COFFEE

¾ CUP POWDERED SUGAR,
  SIFTED (APPROXIMATE)

1 TEASPOON DARK ROAST
  COFFEE BEANS, FINELY
  GROUND

1 To make the brownies, preheat the oven to 325 degrees. Butter an 8-inch square pan.

2 Melt the butter and chocolate in a heavy small saucepan over low heat, stirring occasionally. Whisk in the espresso and cool slightly.

3 In a large mixing bowl, beat the eggs and sugar until light and thick. Blend in the vanilla and the chocolate mixture, and beat until smooth.

4 Stir in the flour. Fold in the nuts, if using, and pour into the prepared pan. Smooth the top of the batter and bake 40 to 45 minutes, or until a toothpick inserted in the center comes out clean. Remove the pan from the oven and cool completely on a wire rack, about 2 hours.

5 To make the frosting, melt the chocolate with the butter. Stir in the espresso. Beat in about ¾ cup powdered sugar, or just enough to make a spreadable, moist icing. Blend in the ground coffee.

6 Frost when cool and chill at least 30 minutes before cutting. Slice into 2-inch squares.

• PRALINE CRISPS •

P raline is made by caramelizing sugar with nuts over direct heat. Here __ coffee beans provide a unique twist to the process. Use blanched almonds, hazelnuts, or macadamias instead of walnuts, if you prefer. The cookies are crisp and chewy at the same time, and they'll keep for weeks if stored properly.

MAKES 20 TO 24

PRALINE

¾ CUP SUGAR

¼ CUP COFFEE BEANS

¼ CUP WALNUTS

CRISPS

2 EGG WHITES, ROOM TEMPER-
ATURE

1¼ CUPS GROUND WALNUTS

3 TABLESPOONS CORNSTARCH,
SIFTED

5 TABLESPOONS POWDERED
SUGAR, SIFTED

1 To make the praline, lightly butter a baking sheet and line it with foil or parchment paper. Butter the liner.

2 Place the sugar, coffee beans, and walnuts in a heavy 9-inch skillet over medium heat and stir occasionally. As the sugar melts, stir until it turns evenly golden in color. Remove from the heat and pour immediately onto the baking sheet. Cool completely and crush to a powder in a food processor. You will have about 1½ cups.

3 To make the crisps, preheat the oven to 375 degrees. Line a baking sheet with foil or parchment paper and lightly butter the liner.

4 Whisk the egg whites until foamy. In a separate bowl blend the ground nuts, cornstarch, and crushed praline. Stir just enough egg white into the nut mixture, kneading lightly if necessary, to form a firm dough.

5 Roll the dough into quarter-size balls and coat them in the powdered sugar, shaking off any excess. If your hands get too sticky forming the cookies, moisten them with water. Place the cookies on the prepared sheet and bake 15 minutes or until the tops are cracked and puffed.

6 Remove to wire racks to cool completely. Store airtight.

• SPICED HAZELNUT-CHOCOLATE •
BISCOTTI

B iscotti are Italian cookies that are delicious dipped in coffee or dessert
wines. Since they are dry and crisp, these confections are an ideal
vehicle for cooking with the coffee bean itself, and they will keep in-
definitely if stored properly. If you prefer almonds to hazelnuts, substitute blanched almonds for the nuts and almond extract for the hazelnut
extract.

MAKES   ABOUT   40

1¾ CUPS ALL-PURPOSE FLOUR

1 CUP SUGAR

⅓ CUP COCOA POWDER

1 TABLESPOON GROUND
CINNAMON

1 TEASPOON FRESHLY GRATED
NUTMEG

½ TEASPOON CLOVES

1 TEASPOON BAKING SODA

4 OUNCES BITTERSWEET CHOC-
OLATE, COARSELY CHOPPED

1 CUP COARSELY CHOPPED
HAZELNUTS

¼ CUP DARK ROAST COFFEE
BEANS, COARSELY CHOPPED

3 LARGE EGGS

1 TEASPOON VANILLA EXTRACT

½ TEASPOON HAZELNUT
EXTRACT

1 Preheat the oven to 350 degrees. Line a cookie sheet with aluminum foil or parchment paper. Lightly grease the liner.

2 In a large bowl sift together the flour, sugar, cocoa powder, cinnamon, nutmeg, cloves, and baking soda. Set aside. Blend in the chocolate, hazelnuts, and coffee beans.

3 Beat the eggs, vanilla, and hazelnut extract in a small bowl, and pour into the dry ingredients. Stir the mixtures thoroughly, kneading if necessary until the dough comes together. The mixture will be stiff. Add 1 to 2 teaspoons water, *only* if necessary.

4 Divide the dough into two equal halves. Lightly flour each half and form each into a 12-inch-long sausage shape. Place the dough on the prepared cookie sheet. Straighten the shapes and brush off any excess flour.

5 Bake for 50 minutes. Remove the strips from the oven and let cool about 10 minutes. Transfer to a cutting board and slice into sharply angled ½-inch slices with a serrated knife. Place the slices cut-side down on a cookie sheet and bake again at 300 degrees about 40 minutes, turning once during the middle of baking. The cookies should be completely dry and crisp. When cooled, store airtight.

• COFFEE PENUCHE •

P enuche is a fudge usually made of brown sugar, butter, cream or
milk, and nuts. Coffee fills in for the cream in this version, giving
the candy an unusual flavor and golden brown color.

MAKES 24 SMALL PIECES

⅔ CUP BREWED DARK ROAST
  COFFEE
2½ CUPS LIGHTLY PACKED
  BROWN SUGAR
3 TABLESPOONS UNSALTED
  BUTTER

1 TEASPOON VANILLA EXTRACT
¾ CUP COARSELY CHOPPED
  PECANS OR WALNUTS

1 Lightly butter a large (8½-by-4½) loaf pan.

2 Stir the coffee and brown sugar in a heavy 2-quart saucepan over
medium heat until the sugar dissolves. Increase the heat and cook without stirring until the mixture reaches 238 degrees on a candy thermometer. Remove from the heat.

3 Add the butter without stirring. When the foam from the candy subsides and the butter begins to melt, stir the mixture occasionally and cool to 100 to 110 degrees. This may take 20 to 30 minutes. Whisk in the vanilla and beat until the mixture starts to thicken (about 5 minutes). Stir in the pecans. Quickly pour into the prepared loaf pan and smooth the top.

4 Cool at least 1 hour. When firm, cut into 24 equal pieces. Store airtight.

· LEMON-SCENTED ESPRESSO · BARS

L emon and espresso have been paired for years, and here the tradition
— continues. These bars will keep a week in the refrigerator or, if well-
wrapped, a month in the freezer.

MAKES 30

CRUST

8 OUNCES UNSALTED BUTTER,
  SOFTENED

1 CUP POWDERED SUGAR

2 CUPS ALL-PURPOSE FLOUR

2 TEASPOONS FRESHLY GRATED
  LEMON ZEST

¼ TEASPOON SALT

FILLING

4 EGGS

1 CUP SUGAR

1 CUP LIGHTLY PACKED BROWN
  SUGAR

¼ CUP BREWED ESPRESSO OR
  DOUBLE-STRENGTH COFFEE,
  ROOM TEMPERATURE

¼ CUP ALL-PURPOSE FLOUR

2 TEASPOONS FRESHLY GRATED LEMON ZEST

3 TO 4 TABLESPOONS DARK ROAST COFFEE BEANS, FINELY GROUND

½ TEASPOON BAKING POWDER

¼ CUP POWDERED SUGAR

1 To make the crust, preheat the oven to 350 degrees. Cream the butter and sugar until light and fluffy. Blend in the flour, lemon zest, and salt. Press the mixture evenly into an ungreased 13-by-9-inch baking dish and bake until light golden brown, 20 to 25 minutes. Remove to a wire rack to cool at least 10 minutes.

2 To make the filling, beat the eggs and sugars in a medium bowl until thick and smooth. Blend in the espresso, flour, lemon zest, ground coffee, and baking powder. Pour over the crust and bake 30 minutes at 350 degrees. Remove to a wire rack to cool completely. Cover, chill, cut into squares, and just before serving, dust with powdered sugar.

EIGHT

FROZEN DESSERTS

• ESPRESSO ICE CREAM •

R obust in flavor and smooth in texture, this ice cream screams for true espresso lovers. For an even stronger taste, use a not-so-fine strainer when separating the coffee grounds and cream.

MAKES 1½ QUARTS

⅔ CUP ESPRESSO OR DARK ROAST COFFEE BEANS, GROUND TO MEDIUM COARSENESS

2 VANILLA BEANS, SPLIT LENGTHWISE

4½ CUPS CREAM

1½ CUPS MILK

12 EGG YOLKS

1⅓ CUPS SUGAR

2 TABLESPOONS BRANDY

1 Blend the espresso beans, vanilla, cream, and milk in a heavy medium saucepan. Bring to a simmer over medium heat, stirring occasionally. Remove the pan from the heat, cover, and allow to steep 15 minutes. Remove and reserve the vanilla bean. Strain the cream into a clean pan, discarding the coffee grounds. Reheat the mixture to a simmer.

2 In a medium bowl, whisk the yolks and sugar until light and fluffy. While whisking, drizzle a cup of the hot cream into the yolks. When well blended, whisk the yolks back into the saucepan with the remaining cream.

3 Continue stirring over low heat until the mixture thickens and coats the back of a spoon. Do not allow the mixture to boil.

4 Strain the custard into a clean metal bowl to cool. Scrape the vanilla bean lengthwise with a small knife to remove the tiny seeds. Stir them into the mixture. Chill the custard in the refrigerator or, preferably, place the bowl over a larger bowl of ice water and whisk until chilled.

5 Add the brandy to the custard and pour it into an ice-cream maker. Follow the manufacturer's instructions for processing. Cover and freeze up to a week.

• FROZEN TIA MARIA TERRINE •

U ltra smooth and creamy, this prizewinning terrine is a snap to pre-
── pare and can be made days ahead of time.

MAKES 10 TO 12 SERVINGS

1 CUP SUGAR

¾ CUP WATER

8 EGG YOLKS

⅓ CUP COFFEE LIQUEUR

1 CUP CREAM

¾ CUP COFFEE LIQUEUR
(OPTIONAL)

1 Line a 7-cup loaf pan with plastic wrap. Set aside.

2 In a heavy small saucepan, bring the sugar and water to a boil, stirring. Boil without stirring 5 minutes. Meanwhile, in a large bowl, beat the egg yolks at high speed until pale and fluffy. Reduce the speed and drizzle in the sugar syrup while beating.

3 When the syrup is incorporated, increase the speed and continue beating to thicken it and to cool the mixture to room temperature (placing the bowl directly over ice water will hasten the chilling).

4 Fold in ⅓ cup coffee liqueur. In a chilled bowl, whip the cream to soft peaks and fold into the yolk mixture. Pour into the prepared loaf pan and cover with plastic wrap. Freeze at least 8 hours.

5 Using the plastic, remove the terrine from the pan. With a warm clean knife, cut one slice at a time and place on chilled individual plates. Pour 1 tablespoon coffee liqueur around each slice, if desired, and serve immediately.

• JAMOCHA-ALMOND-FUDGE • ICE CREAM

C ommercially a longtime favorite, jamocha-almond-fudge ice cream tastes better made at home with pure ingredients. The alcohol in the rum prevents the ice cream from freezing too hard, but it can be eliminated, if preferred.

MAKES 1¼ QUARTS

1½ CUPS MILK

6 EGG YOLKS

1 CUP SUGAR

12 OUNCES BITTERSWEET OR
  SEMISWEET CHOCOLATE,
  GRATED

¾ CUP BREWED DARK ROAST
  COFFEE, COLD

2 CUPS CREAM

1 TABLESPOON VANILLA
  EXTRACT

¼ CUP DARK RUM

1½ CUPS COARSELY CHOPPED,
  TOASTED ALMONDS

1 Bring the milk to a simmer in a heavy medium saucepan. In a large bowl, whisk the egg yolks with the sugar until thick and lemon colored. While the milk is hot, whisk it gradually into the yolks. Return the mixture to the saucepan. Stir over moderate heat until thickened. Do not allow it to boil.

2 Pour the mixture back into the bowl. Stir in the chocolate and whisk until melted. Place over a larger bowl of ice water and whisk occasionally until cool. Blend in the coffee, cream, vanilla, rum, and almonds.

3 Pour into an ice-cream maker and freeze according to the manufacturer's instructions. Cover and freeze up to a week.

. DARK ROAST HAZELNUT . ICE CREAM

*T*wo favorite Italian flavors, dark roast coffee and toasted hazelnuts, highlight this luscious ice cream. The recipe doubles and triples easily.

MAKES ABOUT 1 PINT

1 CUP MILK

1 CUP CREAM

3 TABLESPOONS DARK ROAST COFFEE BEANS, FINELY GROUND

2 EGG YOLKS

½ CUP SUGAR

½ TEASPOON VANILLA EXTRACT

1 CUP COARSELY CHOPPED, TOASTED HAZELNUTS (SEE NOTE BELOW)

1 Stir the milk, cream, and coffee beans over medium heat in a heavy medium saucepan. Bring to a simmer, stirring. Remove from the heat, cover, and let steep 15 minutes. Strain into a clean saucepan and bring back to a simmer.

2 In a medium bowl, beat the egg yolks with the sugar until thickened and smooth. While whisking, drizzle half of the hot cream into the yolks. Add the yolks and cream to the balance of the cream in the saucepan. Cook over low heat, stirring, until the mixture thickens and coats the back of a spoon. Do not allow it to boil.

3 Pour the custard into a metal bowl. Place over a larger bowl filled with ice water. Whisk occasionally until cool, about 10 minutes.

4 Stir in the vanilla and hazelnuts. Pour into an ice-cream maker and freeze according to the manufacturer's instructions. Cover and freeze for up to a week.

NOTE: *TO TOAST HAZELNUTS,* preheat the oven to 350 degrees. Place the hazelnuts on a jelly-roll pan and toast, tossing occasionally, about 20 minutes or until golden brown. Rub between two dishtowels or paper toweling to remove as much loosened skin as possible.

NINE

CAKES AND PIES

• TURKISH DECADENCE •

*D*ivinely rich and moist, this simple-to-prepare, no-flour cake will entice chocoholics and coffee lovers alike. Dark roast coffee beans, ground to a fine, flour-like powder, is traditional for Turkish coffee.

MAKES 16 TO 20 SERVINGS

CAKE

1 POUND SEMISWEET CHOCO-
LATE, CHOPPED

2 CUPS UNSALTED BUTTER

1 CUP BREWED ESPRESSO OR
DOUBLE-STRENGTH DARK
ROAST COFFEE

1 CUP SUGAR

1 CUP LIGHTLY PACKED BROWN
SUGAR

10 EGGS

2 TABLESPOONS DARK ROAST
COFFEE BEANS, FINELY
GROUND

GLAZE

½ CUP BREWED ESPRESSO OR
DOUBLE-STRENGTH DARK
ROAST COFFEE

2 TABLESPOONS LIGHT CORN
SYRUP

12 OUNCES SEMISWEET CHOC-
OLATE, GRATED

1 TEASPOON VANILLA EXTRACT

1 To make the cake, preheat the oven to 250 degrees. Line a 9-by-3-

inch-high round springform pan with foil, covering the sides as well as the bottom of the pan. Press firmly into the bottom angles, smoothing the foil on the sides and over the rim of the pan. Lightly grease the foil.

2 Combine the chocolate, butter, espresso, and the sugars in a large saucepan over medium heat. Stir until the mixture is melted and smooth. Do not allow it to boil. Meanwhile, beat the eggs in a large bowl. While whisking, drizzle in 1 cup of the chocolate mixture, beating vigorously to prevent the eggs from cooking. Whisk in the remaining chocolate mixture and blend in the finely ground coffee.

3 Pour into the prepared pan. Bake 1½ hours. The center will appear uncooked, but the sides will have pulled away from the pan. Remove from the oven and allow to cool on a wire rack. Cover and chill overnight or up to 2 days.

4 To make the glaze, bring the coffee and corn syrup to a simmer in a heavy medium saucepan. Remove from the heat and whisk in the chocolate. When smooth, stir in the vanilla.

5 Remove the cake from the baking pan to a wire rack placed over a large plate. Drizzle the icing over the decadence, smoothing to cover the top and sides. Chill at least one hour, or until ready to serve. To make smooth slivers of cake, slice with a knife that has been dipped in hot water and wiped dry.

· ESPRESSO CREAM ROLL ·

T his stunning favorite delights the eye and offers sharp contrasts in
flavor. The dark chocolate icing encases spirals of vanilla cake and
espresso-laced filling.

MAKES 10 TO 12 SERVINGS

PASTRY CREAM

8 EGG YOLKS

½ CUP SUGAR

⅜ CUP ALL-PURPOSE FLOUR

1½ CUPS CREAM

¾ CUP BREWED ESPRESSO OR
DOUBLE-STRENGTH DARK
ROAST COFFEE

1 3-INCH CINNAMON STICK

CAKE

7 EGGS, ROOM TEMPERATURE

¾ CUP SUGAR

1¼ CUPS CAKE FLOUR

1 TEASPOON BAKING POWDER

¼ TEASPOON SALT

1 TEASPOON VANILLA EXTRACT

2 TABLESPOONS POWDERED
SUGAR

<u>I C I N G</u>

1 ¼ CUPS SUGAR

½ CUP BREWED DARK ROAST
  COFFEE

6 OUNCES SEMISWEET CHOCO-
  LATE, GRATED

1 To make the pastry cream, whisk the egg yolks and the sugar in a medium bowl. Whisk in the flour until completely blended. Heat the cream, espresso, and cinnamon stick over medium heat in a heavy medium saucepan. Bring to a simmer, remove the cinnamon stick, and gradually whisk the cream into the yolks. Return the mixture to the saucepan. Whisk constantly over medium-low heat until the mixture comes to a boil. Continue whisking while the cream boils 1 to 2 minutes. Strain the custard into a bowl, stir, cover, and chill.

2 To make the cake, preheat the oven to 375 degrees. Line a 17-by-11-inch jelly-roll pan with parchment paper or foil. Butter and flour the liner, shaking off any excess. Beat the eggs with the sugar until light and smooth. Sift together the flour, baking powder, and salt. Beat the dry ingredients into the eggs to form a thick batter. Blend in the vanilla.

3 Spread the mixture into the prepared cake pan and bake 8 to 12 minutes, or until the cake springs back when lightly pressed and the top looks golden. Sprinkle a lightweight towel with the powdered sugar and invert the cake onto it. Peel away the parchment or foil and roll the cake with the towel into a spiral from the long side. Cool for 30 minutes.

4 Whisk the pastry cream until smooth. Unroll the cake and spread the cream evenly over it. Reroll the cake and place seam-side down on a serving tray. Trim the ends of the cake, if necessary, and chill at least 4 hours.

5 To make the icing, dissolve the sugar in the coffee in a heavy small saucepan over medium-low heat, stirring until it comes to a simmer. Remove from the heat and immediately whisk in the chocolate. Cool slightly, whisking occasionally. Drizzle evenly over the cake, letting any excess pool around the sides. Chill until set and slice the cake with a serrated knife.

· MOCHA CHEESECAKE ·

A s moist and creamy as imaginable, this cake balances chocolate and coffee flavors perfectly. If well covered and chilled, the cake will keep for a full week.

MAKES ONE 9-INCH CAKE

CRUST

1 ½ CUPS GRAHAM CRACKER
  CRUMBS
¼ CUP SUGAR

6 TABLESPOONS UNSALTED
  BUTTER, SOFTENED

FILLING

8 OUNCES SEMISWEET CHOCO-
  LATE, GRATED
3 TABLESPOONS CREAM
1 ½ POUNDS CREAM CHEESE,
  SOFTENED
1 CUP SUGAR
3 EGGS
1 ½ CUPS SOUR CREAM

½ CUP BREWED ESPRESSO OR
  DOUBLE-STRENGTH DARK
  ROAST COFFEE, COOLED
  SLIGHTLY
2 TEASPOONS VANILLA
  EXTRACT
CHOCOLATE CURLS FOR GAR-
  NISH, OPTIONAL (SEE NOTE
  BELOW)

1 To make the crust, blend the graham cracker crumbs with the sugar and the softened butter. Press evenly onto the bottom of a 9-inch spring-form pan and chill until ready to fill.

2 To make the filling, preheat the oven to 350 degrees. Melt the chocolate and cream in a heavy small saucepan over low heat, stirring constantly. Cool slightly. In the bowl of an electric mixer or a food processor, beat the cream cheese with the sugar until light and smooth. Beat in the eggs, one at a time. Blend in the melted chocolate, sour cream, espresso, and vanilla, and beat until smooth.

3 Pour the mixture into the chilled pan and bake in the center of the preheated oven 60 to 70 minutes. The center of the cake will jiggle, but it will solidify while cooling. Remove the cake from the oven and cool on a wire rack. Chill thoroughly before serving.

4 Remove the springform pan ring and garnish, if desired, with shaved chocolate curls. To serve, slice into very thin wedges with a knife dipped in hot water.

NOTE: *TO MAKE CHOCOLATE CURLS,* melt 2 ounces semisweet chocolate and pour it onto a hard flat surface. When the chocolate has set, hold a sharp knife at a 45-degree angle and push it along the chocolate to form curls. Repeat until all the chocolate is used. Arrange the curls from the center of the cake outward in a spoke pattern.

MACADAMIA MALABAR MOUSSE PIE

*T*his dense crust creates interesting contrast to smooth chocolate and a light mousse filling. Use chocolate wafers in the crust for a triple-chocolate dessert, or use graham crackers for a striking difference in flavor, texture, and color. If macadamias are beyond your budget, substitute pecans or walnuts.

MAKES 8 TO 10 SERVINGS

CRUST

1½ CUPS GRAHAM CRACKER OR CHOCOLATE WAFER CRUMBS

3 TABLESPOONS UNSALTED BUTTER, SOFTENED

3 TABLESPOONS COFFEE LIQUEUR

FILLING

4 OUNCES SEMISWEET CHOCOLATE, GRATED

½ CUP UNSALTED BUTTER

1 RECIPE MOCHA MOUSSE (PAGE 105)

WHIPPED CREAM

COCOA POWDER

8 TO 10 WHOLE MACADAMIA NUTS

1 To make the crust, blend the graham cracker or chocolate wafer crumbs with the butter and liqueur in a medium bowl. Press evenly onto the bottom and sides of a 10-inch pie plate. Chill until ready to fill.

2 To make the filling, melt the chocolate and butter in a heavy small saucepan over medium-low heat. Whisk to blend the mixture, cool it slightly, and pour it over the crust. Swirl the pie plate to coat the sides of the crust. Chill at least 10 minutes.

3 Follow steps 1–5 of Mocha Mousse. Pour the mousse onto the chocolate and butter, and chill at least 3 hours. Garnish with whipped cream, a dusting of cocoa powder, and whole macadamia nuts.

4 To serve, dip a sharp knife into hot water, wipe it dry, and slice into wedges. Serve immediately.

CHOCOLATE-FILLED CHOCOLATE CAKE

*R*ich with three contrasting textures of chocolate, this intriguing cake is also enhanced by three different forms of coffee—brewed espresso, finely ground beans, and coffee liqueur.

MAKES 14 TO 18 SERVINGS

CAKE

2 CUPS ALL-PURPOSE FLOUR

½ CUP COCOA

2 TEASPOONS BAKING SODA

½ TEASPOON SALT

⅔ CUP UNSALTED BUTTER, SOFTENED

1 CUP SUGAR

2 EGGS

1 CUP BUTTERMILK

½ CUP BREWED ESPRESSO OR DOUBLE-STRENGTH DARK ROAST COFFEE, COOLED

1 TEASPOON VANILLA EXTRACT

FILLING

6 OUNCES DARK OR SEMISWEET CHOCOLATE, GRATED

⅓ CUP CREAM

¼ CUP COFFEE LIQUEUR

1 TABLESPOON DARK ROAST COFFEE BEANS, FINELY GROUND

GLAZE

8 OUNCES DARK OR SEMISWEET CHOCOLATE, GRATED   **2 TABLESPOONS VEGETABLE OIL**

1 To make the cake, preheat the oven to 350 degrees. Lightly grease and flour a 9-inch springform pan. Sift the flour, cocoa, baking soda, and salt into a medium bowl. In a large mixing bowl, cream the butter and sugar until light and fluffy. Beat in the eggs, one at a time, mixing well after each addition.

2 Blend the buttermilk, espresso, and vanilla in a small bowl. With the mixer on low speed, add a third of the flour mixture to the butter then half of the liquid, and repeat until all the ingredients are incorporated. Scrape down the sides of the bowl as needed. Mix until just barely blended. Pour the batter into the prepared pan and bake until a toothpick inserted in the center comes out clean, 40 to 45 minutes. Remove to a wire rack to cool completely.

3 Run a sharp knife 2 inches from the edge around the inside of the cake, carefully slicing down to leave the bottom ¾ inch intact. Scoop out this section of cake with a spoon, forming a "bowl" of cake. Mince the cake crumbs and reserve them for the filling.

4 To make the filling, melt the chocolate with the cream in a heavy small saucepan over medium-low heat, stirring occasionally. Pour the chocolate into a mixing bowl and beat until smooth. Stir in the cake crumbs, coffee liqueur, and ground coffee. Pour the filling into the cake, smooth the top, cover and chill until set, at least 3 hours.

5 To make the glaze, place the chocolate in the top of a double boiler over barely simmering water. Stir occasionally until melted. Remove the chocolate from the heat and whisk in the oil. Pour the glaze onto the cake and swirl it over the entire surface with a flat spatula. Smooth the top and sides, and chill the cake. To serve, remove the cake from the refrigerator 15 minutes before slicing into small wedges.

OVEN TEMPERATURE EQUIVALENCIES

DESCRIPTION	°FAHRENHEIT	°CELSIUS
COOL	200	90
VERY SLOW	250	120
SLOW	300–325	150–160
MODERATELY SLOW	325–350	160–180
MODERATE	350–375	180–190
MODERATELY HOT	375–400	190–200
HOT	400–450	200–230
VERY HOT	450–500	230–260

• METRIC CONVERSION TABLE •

LIQUID AND DRY MEASURE EQUIVALENCIES

CUSTOMARY	METRIC
¼ TEASPOON	1.25 MILLILITERS
½ TEASPOON	2.5 MILLILITERS
1 TEASPOON	5 MILLILITERS
1 TABLESPOON	15 MILLILITERS
1 FLUID OUNCE	30 MILLILITERS
¼ CUP	60 MILLILITERS
⅓ CUP	80 MILLILITERS
½ CUP	120 MILLILITERS
1 CUP	240 MILLILITERS
1 PINT (2 CUPS)	480 MILLILITERS
1 QUART (4 CUPS, 32 OUNCES)	960 MILLILITERS (.96 LITERS)
1 GALLON (4 QUARTS)	3.84 LITERS
1 OUNCE (BY WEIGHT)	28 GRAMS
¼ POUND (4 OUNCES)	114 GRAMS
1 POUND (16 OUNCES)	454 GRAMS
2.2 POUNDS	1 KILOGRAM (1000 GRAMS)

INDEX